Only Believe

~Amazing Grace~

By

Stacy Adams

Copyright © 2014 by Stacy Adams

All rights reserved.

ISBN-10: 1499313403

ISBN-13: 978-1499313406

Dedicated to:

The Lord Jesus Christ our healer

Thank you Deb for introducing me to Jesus!

Thank you to all of my family, my husband John, my children and grandchildren, I love you.

This book is also dedicated to my sister Mandy for her questions prompting the start of my book writing journey.

To my friends Maggie and Melissa,

our Thursday night bible study group,

and

everyone and anyone who needs a touch from Jesus!

Thank you Miriah, Patti and Tami for helping with the editing.

TABLE OF CONTENTS

INTRODUCTION

Have you ever wondered if healing is for today or why some people are healed and some remain sick or die? This book represents my journey through the scriptures over the past couple of years.

I am a registered nurse, a Christian and a minister. This has given me the opportunity to view things medically and spiritually. Personally I have been healed of depression, glaucoma and TMJ.

As you read this book, pray the Holy Spirit will open your eyes and heart to the truths of God's word. The scriptures are God's word and authority on healing. If you have any preconceived ideas, opinions or prejudices against healing, set them aside. If you are truly seeking the truth, you will find it.

John 16:13 "However, when He, the Spirit of truth, has come, He will guide you into all truth; for He will not speak on His own authority, but whatever He hears He will speak; and He will tell you things to come."

2 Timothy 3:16-17 All scripture is given by inspiration of God, and is profitable for doctrine, for reproof, for correction, for instruction in righteousness, that the man of God may be complete, thoroughly equipped for every good work.

Jeremiah 33:3 "Call to Me, and I will answer you, and show you great and mighty things, which you do not know."

John 8:32 "And you shall know the truth, and the truth shall make you free."

John 8:36 "Therefore if the Son makes you free, you shall be free indeed."

FIRST THINGS FIRST

GOOD NEWS (The Best You Can Ever Hear)

If you do not know Jesus personally, I would like to introduce Him to you. Jesus is the best friend you can ever have and He will never let you down.

As I grew up I attended a Lutheran church and had friends that attended other churches. I had visited Pentecostal, Catholic, Presbyterian and Methodist churches. All claimed to be right but all were different. This made no sense to me and eventually I came to the conclusion there was no God. The bible says that only a fool says there is no God. I'm not here to argue for or against any religion and I'm not saying that all people in these denominations do not know Jesus, I'm just saying that it made things confusing for me. Religion can make things much more complicated than Jesus intended.

The best place to hide a lie is between two truths. ~ Unknown

Beware of the half truth. You may have gotten hold of the wrong half. ~ Author Unknown

John 8:32 "And you shall know the truth, and the truth shall make you free." ~ Jesus Christ

John 14:6 "I am the way, the truth, and the life. No one comes to the father except through Me." ~ Jesus Christ

1 Corinthians 1:17 "For Christ sent me not to baptize, but preach the gospel, not with wisdom of words, lest the cross of Christ should be made of no effect."

Romans 1:16 For I am not ashamed of the gospel of Christ, for

it is the power of God to salvation for everyone who believes, for the Jew first and also for the Greek.

The word gospel is good news; amazing almost too good to be true news.

RECOGNIZE JESUS HAS A PLAN FOR YOU AND LOVES YOU

Jeremiah 29:11 For I know the thoughts that I think toward you, says the Lord, thoughts of peace and not of evil, to give you a future and a hope.

In John 10:10 Jesus said, "I have come that they may have life, and that they have it more abundantly."

SIN SEPARATES PEOPLE FROM GOD

Romans 3:23 For all have sinned and fall short of the glory of God.

Romans 6:23 For the wages of sin is death, but the gift of God is eternal life in Christ Jesus our Lord.

Romans 3:20 Therefore by the deeds of the law no flesh will be justified in His sight, for by the law is the knowledge of sin.

The bible says everyone is a sinner and sin leads to death. Anything we do to work toward our right standing with God is not enough to save us, that's why Jesus came. Going to church and being a good person does not make you a Christian, knowing Jesus as your Lord and Savior makes you a Christian.

If you believe you will be saved because you follow the Ten Commandments or the law, you are misled. God gave the law so we could see we were sinners and needed a Savior. No one was able to keep the whole law. The bible says if we mess up in one area of the law, we are guilty of all.

James 2:10 For whoever shall keep the whole law, and yet stumble in one point, he is guilty of all.

GOD'S SOLUTION

Isaiah 7:14 "Therefore the Lord Himself will give you a sign: Behold, the virgin shall conceive and bear a Son, and shall call His name Immanuel." *(God with us)*

Romans 5:8 But God demonstrates His own love toward us, in that while we were still sinners, Christ died for us.

1 John 2:2 And He Himself is the propitiation *(atoning sacrifice)* **for our sins, and not for ours only but also for the whole world.**

John 3:3 Jesus answered and said to him, "Most assuredly, I say to you, unless one is born again, he cannot see the kingdom of God."

The first birth is our natural birth into this world. The second birth is a spiritual birth, being born again. Being born again is simply believing in Jesus Christ and receiving Him as your Lord and Savior.

John 3:16-18 "For God so loved the world that He gave His only begotten Son, that whoever believes in Him should not perish but have everlasting life. For God did not send His Son into the world to condemn the world, but that the world through Him might be saved. He who believes in Him is not condemned; but he who does not believe is condemned already, because he has not believed in the name of the only begotten Son of God."

1 Corinthians 15:1-4 Moreover, brethren, I declare to you the

gospel which I preached to you, which also you received and in which you stand, by which also you are saved, if you hold fast that word which I preached to you-unless you believed in vain. For I delivered to you first of all that which I also received: that Christ died for our sins according to the Scriptures, and that He was buried, and that He rose again the third day according to the Scriptures.

GOD'S FREE LOVE GIFT TO YOU

Ephesians 1:7 In Him we have redemption *(freed from sin)* **through His blood, the forgiveness of sins, according to the riches of His grace.**

Ephesians 2:8-9 For by grace you have been saved through faith, and that not of yourselves; it is the gift of God, not of works, lest anyone should boast.

Salvation is a gift from God. Through God's grace, you receive the gift by believing and putting your trust in Him. It is like someone handing you a present, you can receive it or reject it, but you don't have to work for it.

Romans 10:2-4 For I bear them witness that they have a zeal for God, but not according to knowledge. For they being ignorant of God's righteousness, and seeking to establish their own righteousness, have not submitted to the righteousness of God. For Christ is the end of the law for righteousness *(right standing with God)* **to everyone who believes.**

Galatians 2:16 "knowing that a man is not justified *(freed from guilt of sin)* **by the works of the law but by faith in Jesus Christ, even we have believed in Christ Jesus, that we might be justified by faith in Christ and not by the works of the law; for by the works of the law no flesh shall be justified."**

Titus 3:5-7 not by works of righteousness which we have done, but according to His mercy *(compassion)* He saved us, through the washing of regeneration *(made spiritually alive)* and renewing of the Holy Spirit, whom He poured out on us abundantly through Jesus Christ our Savior, that having been justified by His grace we should become heirs according to the hope of eternal life.

Romans 4:4-5 Now to him who works, the wages are not counted as grace but as debt. But to him who does not work but believes on Him who justifies the ungodly, his faith is accounted for righteousness.

Romans 8:3-4 For what the law could not do in that it was weak through the flesh, God did by sending His own Son in the likeness of sinful flesh, on account of sin: He condemned sin in the flesh that the righteous requirement of the law might be fulfilled in us who do not walk according to the flesh but according to the Spirit.

Religion can have us working toward our salvation instead of accepting what Christ did for us on the cross. That kind of faith is useless. We are saved by grace *(God's undeserved favor toward us)* through faith; through Jesus we become righteous or are in right standing with God.

RECEIVE JESUS AS YOUR SAVIOR

Romans 10:9-13 that if you confess with your mouth the Lord Jesus and believe in your heart that God raised Him from the dead, you will be saved. For with the heart one believes unto righteousness, and with the mouth confession is made unto salvation. For the Scripture says, "Whoever believes on Him will not be put to shame." For there is no distinction between

Jew and Greek, for the same Lord over all is rich to all who call upon Him. For "whoever calls on the name of the Lord shall be saved."

Hebrews 8:12 "For I will be merciful to their unrighteousness, and their sins and their lawless deeds I will remember no more."

Romans 2:4 Or do you despise the riches of His goodness, forbearance, and longsuffering, not knowing that the goodness of God leads you to repentance *(a change of mind that results in changes in actions and thinking)*?

Through prayer (talking with Jesus), you can receive Jesus as your Lord and Savior. It is not enough to know about Jesus, you must believe with your heart and know Him personally. Everyone is a sinner and needs a Savior. Accept what Jesus has done for you, it's a free gift that you must receive by faith. You must put your full trust in Jesus for your salvation.

You can pray something like this: Jesus, I know that I am a sinner and I need your forgiveness. I believe you died in my place, paying for my sins. I accept your gift of salvation and ask you to come into my heart and be my Lord and Savior. Amen

If you accepted Jesus as your Lord and Savior, look for a bible believing church to attend, read your bible asking the Holy Spirit to teach you and talk to Jesus every day. Jesus is alive and He wants you to be blessed in everything you do.

CHAPTER 1

IN THE BEGINNING

~

Before I knew Jesus as my Lord, I had a nice family, a good job, a nice house and most people would think a nice life. I was miserable and taking antidepressants. After I had my younger son, the doctor doubled the dose of the antidepressant I was taking and added a second antidepressant. Getting to the point of despair takes time and effort and a lot of practice thinking wrong thoughts, not to mention it is exhausting. I was questioning if I had a purpose in life. I would sit at my desk and cry, wondering if there was any purpose to life because I could not find one. I had tried all sorts of things like shopping, getting remarried more than once, working, alcohol, sex and so on to fill the void in my life. Nothing worked. At this point I was contemplating suicide. I even heard a voice that said, "Just kill yourself." I felt hopeless.

One day I was out interviewing for a new job. While in the parking lot of the first interview, I cried out, "If there is a God, you'd better give me a sign!" I meant it or I was done with life.

When I got to the second interview, the interview I didn't want to go to, Deb, the woman interviewing me, said she had a message that I was to supposed to take the job, but it had nothing to do with a job. Who talks like that at an interview? I knew in my heart, it was God. I knew it was my sign, so I took the job and that's where I met Jesus.

It was only a short time after receiving Jesus as my Lord and Savior that He spoke my heart telling me He was greater than any disease or depression. I knew that I knew, without a doubt, that Jesus was greater. I can't explain how I knew, I just knew. I stopped taking one of the prescriptions antidepressants and then the other. I took a two week vacation. During my time off, I had battles in my mind about going and getting a new prescription. I heard things like, "You need that medication." The thoughts came fast and frequent. On more than one occasion I was almost out the door to get more medication. I had it timed in my mind how long it would take to get to the doctor, have a new prescription written and get it filled at the pharmacy. I felt miserable. To make it through, I kept telling the Lord, "I know you're greater. I know you're greater." At that time, I didn't know very many scriptures about healing, I just knew Jesus was greater. The very last day of my vacation, I knew I was set free. I just started laughing. It was not an easy road, but the Lord is faithful and He is greater than any disease or depression.

I am not suggesting to anyone to stop your medication without a revelation from Jesus. Jesus tells us that if we continue in His word, and hold to His teachings, we will know the truth, and the truth will set us free.

Where did sickness come from?

In Genesis 1:26-28 Adam and Eve were created in God's image according to His likeness. In the Garden of Eden they walked in divine health. Sickness and disease were not part of their lives. God blessed them and told them to fill the earth and subdue it. He also gave them dominion *(power to govern and control)* over the birds, fish, and over every living thing that moves on the earth.

In Genesis 3:1-6 Adam sinned against God and turned dominion over to Satan. **Luke 4:6 says, "And the devil said to Him, 'All this authority I will give You, and their glory; for this has been delivered to me, and I give it to whomever I wish.'"** Through sin, Adam not only handed over dominion but opened the door to the curse. Sickness, disease, poverty, destruction and death are consequences of sin and are listed under curses.

<u>CURSES for disobedience in Deuteronomy 28:15-68 (NIV)</u>
*You will be cursed in the city and cursed in the country
*Your basket and your kneading trough will be cursed
*The fruit of your womb will be cursed
*and the crops of your land,
*and the calves of your herds and the lambs of your flocks
*You will be cursed when you come in and when you go out
*The Lord will plague you with diseases until He has destroyed you from the land you are entering to possess
*The Lord will strike you with wasting disease, with fever and inflammation, with scorching heat and drought, with blight and mildew, which will plague you until you perish
*The sky over your head will be bronze, the ground beneath you iron
*The rain over your land will be dust and powder
*You will be defeated before your enemies
*Your carcasses will be food for all the birds of the air and the beasts of the earth
*The Lord will afflict you with the boils of Egypt and with tumors, festering sores and the itch, from which you

cannot be cured

*You will be afflicted with madness, with blindness and confusion of mind

*You will grope about like a blind man in the dark

*You will be oppressed and robbed

*You will be pledged to be married to a woman, but another will take her and ravish her

*You will build a house, but you will not live in it

*You will plant a vineyard, but you will not even begin to enjoy it's fruit

*Your ox will be slaughtered before your eyes, but you will eat none of it. Your donkey will be forcibly taken from you and will not be returned. Your sheep will be given to your enemies

*Your sons and daughters will be given to another nation

*A people that you do not know will eat what your land and labor produce

*The Lord will afflict your knees and legs with painful boils that cannot be cured, spreading from the soles of your feet to the top of your head

*You will sow much seed in the field but you will harvest little, because locusts will devour it

*The alien who lives among you will rise above you higher and higher, but you will sink lower and lower

*He will lend to you, but you will not lend to him

*He will be the head, but you will be the tail

Disease is in the world because of sin. In the Old Testament, God warned of the consequences of sin and wrong choices. When the people were disobedient curses came upon them. The people had the choice to be obedient or disobedient because God gives us free will. Wrong choices came with negative consequences and right choices with blessings. God did not place the curses on the people but curses came as a consequence of sin (study the Hebrew). God has told us how to live to avoid the troubles of this world, we need to follow what He says or He cannot work in our favor. Satan hopes we make the wrong choices so he can rule in our lives. Satan is the one who brings the curses.

God loves us as we love our children. We teach our children right from wrong but they still make choices. For instance, we may teach our young children to look before crossing the road so they do not get hit by a car. If they are disobedient, we do not push them in front of a car so they get hit but rather, they get hit by the car if they do not look. If they are disobedient and make the wrong choice there can be negative consequences. The same with God's laws, He warns not to do certain things because there are negative consequences. He does not warn us to keep good from us but to keep us safe. God is giving us wisdom to lead a successful life.

Deuteronomy 30:19 "I call heaven and earth as witnesses today against you, that I have set before you life and death, blessing and cursing; therefore choose life, that both you and your descendants may live." God gave a choice between life and death and between blessings and cursing. He tells us what choice to make, but we still have free will to make the wrong choice. **Exodus 15:26 and said, "If you diligently heed the voice of the Lord your God and do what is right in His sight, give ear to His commandments and keep all His statutes, I will put none of these diseases on you which I have brought on the Egyptians. For I am the Lord who heals you."**

*You will be blessed in the city and blessed in the country

*The fruit of your womb will be blessed

*and the crops of your land

*and the young of your livestock-the calves of your herds and the lambs of your flocks

*Your basket and your kneading trough will be blessed

*You will be blessed when you come in and blessed when you go out

*The Lord will grant that the enemies who rise up against you will be defeated before you. They will come at you from one direction but flee from you in seven

*The Lord will send a blessing on your barns and on everything you put your hand to

*The Lord your God will bless you in the land He is giving you

*The Lord will establish you as His holy people

*Then all the peoples on earth will see that you are called by the name of the Lord, and they will fear you

*The Lord will grant you abundant prosperity

*The Lord will open the heavens, the storehouse of His bounty, to send rain on your land in season and to bless all the work of your hands

*You will lend to many nations but will borrow from none

*The Lord will make you the head, not the tail

Some names of God; Adonai (The Lord), Elohim (The All-Powerful One), El Roi (The God Who sees me), El Shaddai (The All Sufficient One), Immanuel (God with us), Jehovah (I Am), Jehovah Rapha (The Lord Who heals), Jehovah-Rohi (The Lord is my Shepherd), Jehovah-Tsidkenu (The Lord our Righteousness), and YHWH (I Am).

The names of Jesus; Almighty (Power of God, nothing is impossible for Him), Messiah (Anointed one), Redeemer (Guarantee, redeems us from the debt we owe to God's law), Resurrection and the Life (Living One, He is Life), Savior (Deliverer, Salvation), Shepherd (Good Shepherd), Son of God (Son of the Most High, He is Divine), The Way, The Truth, and The Life (Path to God), Bread of Life (Living Bread, Living Water), Bright Morning Star (Light of the World).

In both the Old and New Testaments God healed people. **In Numbers 21: 8-9 Then the Lord said to Moses, "Make a fiery serpent, set it on a pole; and it shall be that everyone who is bitten, when he looks at it, shall live." So Moses made a bronze serpent, put it on a pole; and so it was, if a serpent had bitten anyone, when he looked at the bronze serpent, he lived.** This was a foreshadow of **John 3:14-15 And as Moses lifted up the serpent in the wilderness, even so the Son of Man must be lifted up, that whoever believes in Him should not perish but have eternal life.**

Psalm 103:2-5 Bless the Lord, O my soul, and forget not all His benefits: Who forgives all your iniquities, Who heals all your diseases, Who redeems your life from destruction, Who crowns you with lovingkindness and tender mercies, Who satisfies your mouth with good things, so that your youth is renewed like the eagle's.

Psalm 107:19-20 Then they cried out to the Lord in their trouble, and He saved them out of their distresses. He sent His word and healed them, and delivered them from their destructions.

God is a good God and God has good plans for us.

Jeremiah 29:11 For I know the thoughts that I think toward you, says the Lord, thoughts of peace and not of evil, to give you a future and a hope.

Isaiah 53:4-5 (Hebrew interpretation: One New Man Bible) Surely He has borne our sicknesses, our pains; He carried them, yet we esteemed Him stricken, smitten of God and afflicted. But He was wounded because of our transgressions, bruised because of our iniquities: the chastisement of our peace was upon Him, and we have been healed by His wounds.

In Psalm 103, God says He heals **ALL** of our diseases. What does "all" mean to you? God has been the healer since the beginning and healing continues today. His name is Jehovah Rapha: The Lord Who Heals. So why are there so many sick people including Christians? As we go forward we will uncover some truths in God's word.

CHAPTER 2

THE GREAT DEBATES

~

By His stripes you are healed: Spiritual healing or physical healing?

Isaiah 53:4-5 Surely He has borne our griefs and carried our sorrows; yet we esteemed Him stricken, smitten by God, and afflicted. But He was wounded for our transgressions, He was bruised because for our iniquities; the chastisement for our peace was upon Him, and by His stripes we are healed.

There has been some debate whether or not Isaiah 53:4-5 is talking about spiritual healing or if it is talking about physical healing. The word griefs in Isaiah translates in the Hebrew as sickness.

Matthew 8:16-17 When evening had come, they brought to Him many who were demon-possessed. And He cast out the spirits with a word, and healed all who were sick, that it might be fulfilled which was spoken by Isaiah the prophet, saying: "He Himself took our infirmities and bore our sicknesses."

1 Peter 2:24 who Himself bore our sins in His own body on the tree, that we, having died to sins, might live for righteousness-by whose stripes you were healed (Isaiah 53:5). In 1 Peter 2:24, the same Greek word for "healed" is used in Matthew 8:8, 13; Luke 6:19, 7:7, 9:42; and Mark 5:29.

Matthew 8:8 The centurion answered and said, "Lord, I am not worthy that You should come under my roof. But only speak a word, and my servant will be healed."

Matthew 8:13 Then Jesus said to the centurion, "Go your way; and as you have believed, so let it be done for you." And his servant was healed that same hour.

Luke 6:19 And the whole multitude sought to touch Him, for power went out from Him and healed them all.

Luke 7:7 Therefore I did not even think myself worthy to come to You. But say the word, and my servant will be healed.

Luke 9:42 And as he was still coming, the demon threw him down and convulsed him. Then Jesus rebuked the unclean spirit, healed the child, and gave him back to his father.

Mark 5:29 Immediately the fountain of her blood was dried up, and she felt in her body that she was healed of the affliction.

In 1 Peter 2:24, Peter is quoting from the context of Isaiah 53. Some believe Isaiah 53:4-5 and 1 Peter 2:24 refers to sins are forgiven and spiritual healing, not physical healing. Even if this were true, when our sins are forgiven sickness has no legal right to be in our bodies. Sickness came as a result of sin. Sickness is part of the curse and Christ redeemed *(bought us back)* us from the curse.

1 John 2:2 And He Himself is the propitiation *(atoning sacrifice)* for our sins, and not for ours only but also for the whole world.

Galatians 3:13 Christ has redeemed us from the curse of the law, having become a curse for us (for it is written, "Cursed is everyone who hangs on a tree").

Saved, Healed, Delivered

Sozo is the Greek word that means saved, healed and delivered. It means to be made whole in every way. Sozo is more than just salvation, it includes healing. Sometimes it is translated, saved and others healed or made well, it is a package deal.

Romans 10:9 That if you confess with your mouth the Lord Jesus and believe in your heart that God raised Him from the dead you will be saved (sozo).

Ephesians 2:4-9 But God, who is rich in mercy, because of His great love with which He loved us, even when we were dead in trespasses, made us alive together with Christ (by grace you have been saved 'sozo'), and raised us up together, and made us sit together in the heavenly places in Christ Jesus, that in the ages to come He might show the exceeding riches of His grace in His kindness toward us in Christ Jesus, for by grace you have been saved (sozo) **through faith, and that not of yourselves; it is the gift of God, not of works, lest anyone should boast.**

Think about God's love, mercy and grace in Ephesians 2:4-9. If you love someone, you would want them well. The Lord says in **Matthew 7:11 "If you then, being evil, know how to give good gifts to your children, how much more will your Father who is in heaven give good things to those who ask Him!"**

The word saved (sozo) includes healing and wholeness. Your healing comes the same way our salvation does, by grace through faith. You don't have to do anything to work for it, it's a gift, just receive it by faith.

Matthew 9:22 But Jesus turned around, and when He saw her He said, "Be of good cheer, daughter; your faith has made you well (sozo)." **And the woman was made well from that hour.**

Sozo (italicized words) is found in the following scriptures: **Mark 5:34 And He said to her, "Daughter, your faith has *made* you *well*. Go in peace, and be healed of your affliction." Luke 8:48 And He said to her, "Daughter, be of good cheer, your faith has *made* you *well*. Go in peace."**

Sozo was also used in **James 5:15 And the prayer of faith will *save* the sick, and the Lord will raise him up. And if he has committed sins, he will be forgiven. John 3:17 "For God did not send His Son into the world to condemn the world, but that the world through Him might be *saved*."**

Forgiveness of sins and healing went hand in hand in Jesus ministry. **Mark 2:9 "Which is easier, to say to the paralytic, 'Your sins are forgiven you,' or to say, 'Arise, take up your bed and walk'?"**

When Jesus was beaten and died on the cross, He provided for our salvation, deliverance and physical healing. Christ redeemed us from the curse. Sickness is a curse and is a work of the devil (Acts 10:38). Jesus came to destroy the works of the devil.

1 John 3:8 He who sins is of the devil, for the devil has sinned from the beginning. For this purpose the Son of God was manifested, that He might destroy the works of the devil.

John 10:10 "The thief does not come except to steal, and to kill, and to destroy. I (Jesus) **have come that they may have life, and that they may have it more abundantly."**

Sickness and disease are not abundant life. We need to know clearly which attributes are from God and which ones are from the devil. God is a good God and wants the very best for us. He wants us whole spiritually, emotionally and physically; living a full abundant life.

Jesus offers us many benefits. We will miss out on His benefits if we do not know that they exist, misunderstand them or if we choose to reject them. For instance, Jesus died for the sins of the whole world but not all receive the benefit of salvation. Jesus has already provided for your healing, but if you do not know healing is yours, choose to doubt or reject healing you will not receive it.

Jesus said in **Matthew 10:8, "Heal the sick, cleanse the lepers, raise the dead, cast out demons. Freely you have received, freely give."** The disciples were told to give what they had freely received. They were to heal the sick so they must have received healing as a benefit.

Acts 3:6 Then Peter said, "Silver and gold I do not have, but what I do have I give you; In the name of Jesus Christ of Nazareth, rise up and walk." Peter said to the lame man he would give him what he had. Peter must have received healing in the atonement as this is what he gave to the lame man.

Jesus gave His life for us so we could be made whole in every way; saved, healed, delivered, made whole and prosperous. God loves us and wants the very best for us. God is love. If you can see God the Father as a parent who wants the best for His children as you would want the best for yours, then you will begin to see that God would never want us to be sick, go to hell, struggle or lack anything good. It's actually ridiculous to think a loving God would not want us healed. John 14:6 says that Jesus is the way the truth and the life. God has provided the way, we just have to cooperate with Him through faith.

Paul's Thorn

Paul's thorn has been another area of debate when it comes to healing. Some believe Paul's thorn was a physical sickness. The scripture states Paul's thorn in his flesh was "a messenger of Satan to buffet" him. Buffet means to strike, or contend against. The scripture does not say "sickness". The Greek word translated as messenger always refers to someone who is sent, either by God, man or by Satan; in Paul's case, a messenger of Satan.

2 Corinthians 12:7-9 And lest I should be exalted above measure by the abundance of the revelations, a thorn in the flesh was given to me, a messenger of Satan to buffet me, lest I be exalted above measure. Concerning this thing I pleaded with the Lord three times that it might depart from me. And He said to me, "My grace is sufficient for you, for My strength is made perfect in weakness." Therefore most gladly I will rather boast in my infirmities (Greek word means weakness) **that the power of Christ may rest upon me.**

In Galatians 4:13 infirmity translates weakness as it does in 2 Corinthians 12:9. Paul's weakness or infirmities were more than likely from the beatings he took. Remember he was stoned and left for dead. In Matthew 8:17, Acts 28:9, and John 11:4, infirmity is translated sickness. Matthew 8:17, is in reference to Isaiah 53:4 when Jesus took our infirmities and bore our sicknesses.

We may not be able to produce results in our weaknesses but weaknesses are no longer a problem when we learn to rely on the power and grace of God. When Paul relied on the power of God's grace, he was delivered. God's grace isn't just enough to get by; it's more than enough in any situation. It truly is amazing grace.

The Lord never said Paul did not have power over his thorn in the flesh. He told Paul that in his weakness (infirmity), the Lord's power would be made perfect. The Lord's Grace was more than enough to handle the problem. In 2 Timothy 3:11 Paul says the Lord delivered him out of *ALL* of the persecutions and afflictions.

The Lord never refused to help Paul, He gave Paul the grace to be victorious. In **2 Timothy 3:11 Paul said, "persecutions, afflictions, which happened to me at Antioch, at Iconium, at Lystra-what persecutions I endured, and out of them all the Lord delivered me."**

In 2 Corinthians 11:24-26 Paul had been imprisoned, stoned, beaten, and shipwrecked. These are some of the strikes he took and I am sure he had pain and physical injuries with the beatings.

Numbers 33:55 'But if you do not drive out the inhabitants of the land from before you, then it shall be that those whom you let remain shall be irritants in your eyes and thorns in your sides, and they shall harass you in the land where you dwell.'

Ezekiel 28:24 "And there shall no longer be a pricking brier or a painful thorn for the house of Israel from among all who are around them, who despise them. Then they shall know that I am the Lord God."

In the previous scriptures in Numbers and Ezekiel there are other statements similar to "thorn in the flesh"; "irritants in your eyes", "thorns in your sides", "pricking briers", and "painful thorns". Today we may call it a "pain in the neck". Paul's thorn in the flesh was a messenger sent by Satan not a sickness.

God is love and in no way does a loving God place sickness on someone or refuse to heal someone. This needs to be settled in your heart. If you are looking to be healed, stop looking for scriptures to support or justify sickness. Start meditating on the truth of God's word. God wants you well.

Understanding Communion

1 Corinthians 11:23-30 For I received from the Lord that which I also delivered to you: that the Lord Jesus on the same night in which He was betrayed took bread; and when He had given thanks, He broke it and said, "Take, eat, this is My body which is broken for you; do this in remembrance of Me." In the same manner He also took the cup after super, saying, "This cup is the new covenant in My blood. This do, as often as you drink it, in remembrance of Me." For as often as you eat this bread and drink this cup, you proclaim the Lord's death till He comes. Therefore whoever eats this bread or drinks this cup of the Lord in an unworthy (worthless) **manner will be guilty of the body and blood of the Lord. But let a man examine himself, and so let him eat of the bread and drink of the cup. For he who eats and drinks in an unworthy manner eats and drinks judgment to himself, not discerning the Lord's body. For this reason many are weak and sick among you, and many sleep.**

Paul is not saying unworthy people, he is saying in an unworthy *(worthless)* manner. Remember Jesus' sacrifice, meditate on it. Jesus body (bread) was beaten for our sickness and pain and crucified, shedding His blood (wine) for our sins. In communion the bread represents His body was broken so that we might have life and health. The wine represents His shed blood that we might have forgiveness of our sins. If you do not understand Jesus sacrifice of His body, you are eating in an unworthy or worthless manner. It will not do you any good. The bible says for this reason many are weak and sick among you, and many sleep.

Examine yourself: what is your attitude and belief toward what Christ did for us? Do you have a revelation of Christ's sacrifice? When discerning *(perceiving)* the Lord's body, you need to recognize His full sacrifice (sozo) for us. Think on what Jesus has done for you, the finished work at Calvary (healed, saved and delivered).

Isaiah 53:4-5 Surely He has borne our griefs (*Hebrew: sickness*) **and carried our sorrows** (*Hebrew: pain*)**; yet we esteem Him stricken, smitten by God, and afflicted. But He was wounded for our transgressions, He was bruised for our iniquities; the chastisement for our peace was upon Him, and by His stripes we are healed.**

Matthew 26:26-28 And as they were eating, Jesus took bread, blessed and broke it, and gave it to the disciples and said, "Take, eat, this is My body." Then He took the cup, and gave thanks, and gave it to them, saying, "Drink from it, all of you. For this is My blood of the new covenant, which is shed for many for the remission of sins."

Hebrews 10:12-17 But this man, after He had offered one sacrifice for sins forever, sat down at the right hand of God, from that time waiting till His enemies are made His footstool. For by one offering He has perfected forever those who are being sanctified. But the Holy Spirit also witnesses to us; for after He had said before, "This is the covenant that I will make with them after those days, says the Lord: I will put My laws into their hearts, and in their minds I will write them," then He adds, "Their sins and their lawless deeds I will remember no more."

Hebrews 3:19; 4:1-3 So we see that they could not enter in because of unbelief. Therefore, since a promise remains of

entering His rest, let us fear lest any of you seem to have come short of it. For indeed the gospel was preached to us as well as to them; but the word which they heard did not profit them, not being mixed with faith in those who heard it. For we who have believed do enter that rest, as He has said: "So I swore in My wrath, 'They shall not enter My rest,'" although the works were finished from the foundation of the world.

Listen to and believe God's word, mix it with faith and it will benefit you. Christ's sacrifice is a finished work. Jesus said in John 19:30, "It is finished." Jesus is not up in heaven taking a beating every time someone needs to be healed, just as He is not getting crucified over and over each time someone is getting saved; it is already done. Christ's work is a finished work. There is nothing more He needs to do.

CHAPTER 3

WE ARE AT WAR

~

We have a real enemy

We are all in a spiritual battle and the battle starts in the mind. Think about the thoughts that come through your mind, not all of them are your thoughts. The enemy (devil) brings thoughts and he hopes you receive them as yours. If you have thoughts that are evil, fearful, depressed, anxious, or thoughts that lead to your defeat, they are from the enemy. You do not need to receive them as yours. The thoughts you have and where they take you, the words you speak and what you believe in your heart determine if you are victorious or if you are defeated.

1 Peter 5:8 Be sober, be vigilant; because your adversary the devil walks about like a roaring lion, seeking whom he may devour.

The devil is looking for someone to believe his lies so he can destroy them. Don't fall for his deceptions. You do not have to accept every bad thought or circumstance that is thrown your way.

2 Corinthians 10:3-5 For though we walk in the flesh, we do not war according to the flesh. For the weapons of our warfare are not carnal but mighty in God for pulling down strongholds, casting down arguments and every high thing that exalts itself

against the knowledge of God, bringing every thought into captivity to the obedience of Christ,

The Lord has given us weapons to be victorious against the enemy. One way to defeat the enemy is to cast down any thought that doesn't line up with God's word. That means to change your thinking in your favor by thinking on something good. Do not dwell on the negative thought or it will become yours.

Weapon #1: Armor of God

Ephesians 6:10-17 Finally, my brethren, be strong in the Lord and in the power of His might. Put on the whole armor of God, that you may be able to stand against the wiles of the devil. For we do not wrestle against flesh and blood, but against principalities, against powers, against the rulers of the darkness of this age, against spiritual hosts of wickedness in the heavenly places. Therefore take up the whole armor of God, that you may be able to withstand in the evil day, and having done all, to stand. Stand therefore, having girded your waist with truth, having put on the breastplate of righteousness, and having shod your feet with the preparation of the gospel of peace; above all, taking the shield of faith with which you will be able to quench all the fiery darts of the wicked one. And take the helmet of salvation, and the sword of the Spirit, which is the word of God.

Weapon #2: Word of God and Prayer are Weapons

John 1:1 In the beginning was the Word, and the Word was with God, and the Word was God.

Hebrews 4:12 For the word of God is living and powerful, and

sharper than any two-edged sword, piercing even to the division of soul and spirit, and joints and marrow, and is a discerner of the thoughts and intents (understanding) of the heart.

Isaiah 55:11 So shall My word be that goes forth from My mouth; it shall not return to Me void, but it shall accomplish what I please, and it shall prosper in the thing for which I sent it.

Psalm 107:20 He sent His word and healed them, and delivered them from their destructions.

I had TMJ and was healed. My jaw used to crack when I would chew, get locked into a position and I would not be able to open my mouth, it was painful all the way up the side of my face. I was at the hospital getting ready to discharge home after the birth of our daughter. The T.V. was on in the room and Marilyn Hickey was preaching. She said, "Someone is getting healed of TMJ right now." I knew it was me. I've been healed since. This is an example of God sending forth His word.

I was also healed of glaucoma. I was about thirty when I was diagnosed with glaucoma. The eye doctor said that it was bad enough that I would need to use eye drops by the time I was forty. I met Jesus when I was thirty-four and was healed a short time after from the glaucoma. I was again listening to someone preaching on T.V. and heard a word of knowledge that someone was getting healed of glaucoma, it was me.

If you know the word of God, the devil will not be able to deceive you. Many things come against us in life such as our own bad decisions, sickness, abuse, hurtful words, financial troubles and on and on. If Satan can get us to believe his lies, he can defeat us. He can use wrong teachings, feelings and emotions, physical symptoms, our circumstances, fear and intimidation against us. The devil is defeated and he knows it. He just hopes we don't know it. With Jesus there is always hope. Speak God's promises over your circumstance. Pray the answer, not the problem.

Jesus used the word of God to battle when he was tempted by the devil. **Matthew 4: 3-4** says: **Now when the tempter came to Him, he said, "If You are the Son of God, command that these stones become bread." But He answered and said, "It is written, 'Man shall not live by bread alone, but by every word that proceeds from the mouth of God.' "**

Weapon #3: Love and Forgiveness are Weapons

1 Corinthians 13:3-8 And though I bestow all my goods to feed the poor, and though I give my body to be burned, but have not love, it profits me nothing. Love suffers long and is kind; love does not envy; love does not parade itself, it is not puffed up; does not behave rudely, does not seek its own, is not provoked, thinks no evil; does not rejoice in iniquity, but rejoices in the truth; bears all things, believes all things, hopes all things, endures all things. Love never fails.

A few years ago, my husband John and I had our friend Wayne over for bible study. Wayne had brought a friend of his to join us. My first thought about his friend Steve was repulsion. This was the immediate thought that came to me. Steve was just introduced and had not done one thing wrong. I knew this was absolutely wrong thinking and therefore, I had not received the thought as my own. The bible says that I am to love everyone. Love was definitely not even close to my thoughts. Little did I know, my husband was having the same thoughts.

Steve had coke bottle glasses, a large print bible and could not see to read. He said he had to go back to the eye doctor because his eyes were so bad. Now at this point both my husband and I are silently speaking to the Lord asking Him to show us how to love this repulsive guy.

There were snacks on the table and Steve was digging in with his black fingernails. He had food up and down his sleeve. My husband got up to get more snacks and a cloth to wipe Steve's sleeve. My husband said, "If Jesus can wash feet, I can wash your sleeve." As the night went on, the thoughts of disgust and repulsion left and were replaced with a love for Steve.

When we were praying, we prayed for Steve's eyes to be healed. Immediately after prayer, he could see enough to read his bible with his glasses on. The next morning Wayne called and said that Steve had his full sight and didn't even need his glasses. I believe if the devil could have got us to believe his lies, we would not have seen Steve's eyes healed nor had a new friend.

1 John 4:16 says that God is love. If the devil can get us out of love, he wins because our faith works through love.

Galatians 5:6 For in Christ Jesus neither circumcision nor uncircumcision avails anything, but faith working through love.

Weapon #4: Joy, Praise and Thankfulness are Weapons

Psalm 150:6 Let everything that has breath praise the Lord. Praise the Lord!

Philippians 4:6 Be anxious for nothing, but in everything by prayer and supplication, with thanksgiving, let your requests be known to God;

If we are praising God, we can't be complaining and grumbling about negative things.

I had a time after being delivered from depression that I could feel depression begin to move in on me again. I heard the Lord say, "Praise your way out of it. Praise your way out of it." I put on a CD of praise and worship music and just began to thank the Lord. Within ten minutes, all of the feelings of depression left. The bible says that the joy of the Lord is our strength.

Remember the Israelites desert experience? By direct route, the trip from Egypt to Canaan was not more than 250 miles. Why did it take the Israelites 40 years to complete the trip? The Israelites complained, grumbled, were disobedient and in unbelief. It's to our benefit to praise God and believe His promises, it shortens the trip.

Weapon #5: Authority is a Weapon

Jesus has given us His authority *(enforce obedience)* to do His works on this earth. The devil and sickness must obey the word of God when spoken in authority.

Mark 16:17-18 And these signs will follow those who believe: In My name they will cast out demons; they will speak with new tongues; they will take up serpents; and if they drink anything deadly, it will by no means hurt them; they will lay hands on the sick, and they will recover.

Luke 9:1 Then He called His twelve disciples together and gave them power and authority over all demons, and to cure diseases.

Matthew 10:7-8 And as you go, preach, saying, "The kingdom of heaven is at hand." Heal the sick, cleanse the lepers, raise

the dead, cast out demons. Freely you have received, freely give.

John 14:12 Most assuredly, I say to you, he who believes in Me, the works that I do he will do also; and greater works than these he will do, because I go to My Father.

Knowing who you are in Jesus and the authority you've been given is essential for victory. The Lord does not tell us to beg for answered prayers, He says to speak to your mountain. The Lord says He has given us the authority and we are to use it. We are to take authority over our circumstances, we are to order our circumstances to obey God's word.

Weapon #6: Faith is a Weapon

Believe and trust God's word. The shield of faith quenches the fiery darts (negative thoughts, symptoms of disease, negative words, or circumstances) of the evil one. If you are anxious and fearful, you are not in faith.

Hebrews 11:1 Now faith is the substance of things hoped for, the evidence of things not seen.

Hebrews 11:6 But without faith it is impossible to please Him, for he who comes to God must believe that He is, and that He is a rewarder of those who diligently seek Him. If you are diligently *(persistently)* seeking Him, you will find Him. You will receive the reward.

Jeremiah 29:13 And you will seek Me and find Me, when you search for Me with all your heart.

God spoke to me one day, saying, "I'm not moved by your tears, I'm moved by your faith." I knew immediately that I was just feeling badly for myself and was not in faith. I stopped crying and began to line my thinking up with the word of God, speaking His promises and He took care of the situation once again. Crying, worrying, grumbling, getting angry and feeling badly for yourself does not get prayers answered.

It is not that God does not want to help us nor does He enjoy seeing us struggle. God has done His part through Jesus, our part is to believe Him and use the authority He has given us. God cannot help us unless we cooperate with Him through faith in His word. Crying and feeling badly for ourselves is not faith. The answers to our prayers are waiting for us, we need faith for them to manifest physically. When we are in faith, we are fully assured and confident we have what we asked even though we cannot perceive it with our five senses. We are to pray the promise, not the problem and believe it is done.

Faith = Trust

Trust in God's promises produces answered prayers.

CHAPTER 4

YOUR THOUGHTS CONTROL YOUR LIFE

~

Do your circumstances seem bigger than God?

When we are going through tough circumstances they can seem overwhelming. Circumstances can be physical sickness, family problems, emotional stresses, mental illnesses or financial troubles. If the devil can keep you focused on your problem, he can defeat you. The more we focus on the circumstances, the bigger they become, seeming even too big for God to handle. The opposite is also true, the more you focus on God's word, the smaller your circumstance becomes. To be victorious over your circumstance, you need to be rooted and grounded in the word of God believing His promises. Focus on God's word and not the circumstance. Get your eyes on Jesus, not the problem. Trust God, He is faithful.

Hebrews 10:23 Let us hold fast to the confession of our hope without wavering, for He who promised is faithful.

The key here is not to waver or doubt. Hold fast to what God says without wavering.

John 16:33 "These things I have spoken to you, that in Me you may have peace. In the world you will have tribulation; but be of good cheer, I have overcome the world."

Jesus has the answer for every circumstance we go through. We can have complete peace going through any problem if we trust God. Jesus said He overcame *(to defeat; victorious)* the world.

Philippians 4:6-9 Be anxious for nothing, but in everything by prayer and supplication, with thanksgiving, let your requests be known to God; and the peace of God, which surpasses all understanding, will guard your hearts and minds through Christ Jesus. Finally, brethren, whatever things are true, whatever things are noble, whatever things are just, whatever things are pure, whatever things are lovely, whatever things are of good report, if there is any virtue and if there is anything praiseworthy-meditate on these things.

Notice the Lord says "to be anxious for nothing". Nothing means nothing. We are not to be anxious or worried over anything, not even a diagnosis of terminal illness. When we are fearful or anxious it's because we are allowing our mind to dwell on negative thoughts. When we are worried, we are not in agreement with God, we are in agreement with the devil.

God also says to pray with thanksgiving. Truthfully, being thankful may not always be our first thought when we are facing terrible circumstances. When God says pray with thanksgiving, it's not that we are to be thankful for the problem but thankful to God that He has provided the answer and has delivered us from the problem. If you do not know the word of God for yourself, you will not know what He promised and what His answers is. Remember, it's the truth you know that sets you free.

It is important to notice if we follow the first instructions God gives in Philippians 4:6 to be anxious for nothing, He then says in verse 7 that His peace will guard our hearts and minds. When we trust in God, His peace protects our hearts and minds.

Satan does not have control over you, your thoughts or your circumstances unless you allow him to. Remember Jesus has already defeated the devil so we can be victorious in every situation and over every circumstance, having the abundant life Jesus promised. Yes, I did say we can be victorious over every circumstance.

We have a real enemy, Satan. The devil may use any of the following against you: insecurities, fear, anxiety, unworthiness, imaginations of the worst case scenario, physical symptoms, thinking people are against us, haunted or bound by our past, past failures, not smart enough, no purpose, feeling sorry for yourself, poor pitiful me, everyone has it better than me, no one likes me, alone/lonely, guilt, shame, condemnation, hopelessness and past abuses. These are lies from the enemy. You will be defeated if you believe these lies and you cannot move into your future dragging your past.

Satan: **John 8:44 You are of your father the devil, and the desires of your father you want to do. He was a murderer from the beginning, and does not stand in the truth, because there is no truth in him. When he speaks a lie, he speaks from his own resources, for he is a liar and the father of it.**

When circumstances come against you, do not fall into the trap of the enemy through his lies. There is hope in every situation. Jesus is the answer. Do not dwell on the problem but on the answer. Keep your eyes on Jesus. If you follow feelings and emotions which do not line up with God's word, you will be defeated. In **2 Corinthians 10:3-5** says, "**For though we walk in the flesh, we do not war according to the flesh. For the weapons of our warfare are not carnal but mighty in God for**

pulling down strongholds, casting down arguments and every high thing that exalts itself against the knowledge of God, bringing every thought into captivity to the obedience of Christ," This is telling us to take control of our thoughts, do not let them take control of you. Get rid of all thoughts that do not agree with God's word and replace it with a word from God, meditate on good things. If you are feeling badly for yourself, stop it! It doesn't produce positive outcomes.

Everyone gets thoughts and every problem starts with a thought. If you do not have a negative thought about a circumstance, it's not a problem. Not all thoughts are yours, the devil can place thoughts in our minds. It's what you do or do not do with the thought that determines your outcome. Are you going to agree with the negative thought or get rid of it? If you agree with the negative thought, it has just become yours. If you get rid of the negative thought and align your thinking with God's answers, you will be victorious. God tells us to meditate on good things, not to meditate on or imagine bad things. When you meditate on negative or bad things, you are agreeing with Satan, and he is happy to give you what you are believing for.

I have worked at a toenail clinic once a month for a few years. Sitting and bending for eight to nine hours at a time was causing me to get muscle soreness in my back and legs which would last a couple of days. I found myself thinking about the pain and waiting to wake up the next day hurting before it ever happened. Driving home one night after the clinic the Lord spoke to me, saying, "Stop expecting the pain." That night I stopped expecting the pain, thanked the Lord He took care of the pain and have not had the pain since. Before that, I was seeking pain and receiving pain. The bible says seek and you shall find. I was seeking the wrong thing, pain. I now seek relief.

Earlier we established that the devil is a defeated enemy. Jesus stripped him of all of his authority. Jesus has given us all authority. So if this is true, why does the devil seem to have the upper hand over us? It's simple, we give him our authority through fear, worry, strife and complaining. We open the door to the devil and basically invite him into our lives through doubt, unbelief, and fear.

Matthew 8:13 The Jesus said to the centurion, "Go your way; and as you have believed, so let it be done for you." And his servant was healed that same hour.

Matthew 7:7-8 "Ask, and it will be given to you; seek, and you will find; knock and it will be opened to you. For everyone who asks receives, and he who seeks finds, and to him who knocks it will be opened."

Make sure you are believing for and seeking the right things. Many times people are believing for the worst and receive it. Seeking the worst and receive it. Anytime we are believing contrary to God's word, we open the door for Satan to come into our circumstances. If you dwell on something long enough, you very well may receive it. Think about what you are thinking on or imagining, make sure it is not contrary to God's word.

Proverbs 4:23 tells us to guard our hearts because the issues of life flow out of it. In the NLT translation it says, "Guard your heart above all else, for it determines the course of your life." What you believe in your heart determines the course of your life. It determines if you are victorious or defeated. If you belong to Jesus, you should always be victorious, but too many times we settle for defeat. If you are willing to tolerate what the devil hands out, you will never get rid of it.

Proverbs 23:7 For as he thinks in his heart, so is he.

If you identify with discouragement, your illness, doubt, self pity and depression, it can enslave you the rest of your life. Stop justifying your anger, negative feelings, your sickness and depression. Stop planning the next sickness you are going to get. Stop blaming others. We cannot control others but we can control how we respond to them. Stop confessing how much power other people or your circumstances have over your life and start telling your circumstance how big your God is. Tell your problem that God is on your side and no one can be against you.

Romans 8:31 What then shall we say to these things? If God is for us, who can be against us?

You have control over your emotions, don't let them control you. Our emotions and feelings can lie to us. If you are an emotional wreck when a crisis comes against you, you will not be able to pray effectively. If you are continually thinking negative thoughts and speaking out negative confessions, you have given Satan an open door to come in and have freedom in your life. If you are always agreeing with the devil, you will get what he has for you. Don't forget, the devil has come to rob, kill and destroy.

1 Peter 5:8 Be sober, be vigilant; because your adversary the devil walks about like a roaring lion, seeking whom he may devour.

If you start meditating on God's word and begin to confess what He says and begin to say who He says you are, things will begin to turn around. Begin to see yourself as God sees you. Don't let your emotions run your life. If you feel depressed, think on something good, confess God's word over yourself and move forward with your day. Choose to have a good day. Psalm 118:24 says to rejoice and be glad in the day. It's a choice. No one else is responsible for your happiness. Stop making excuses why you can't have a good day. "You just don't know what I've been through." "You don't know what that person did to me." "If you went through what I've been through you'd be depressed too." Stop justifying. Stop expecting the worst. Begin to expect good things. God has given us power over every situation.

If you are depressed or discouraged, it's because you've submitted to those feelings. You have made the wrong choice. You cannot lead a victorious life being depressed, feeling defeated by illness, feeling sorry for yourself or discouraged. None of this is written to condemn you but to encourage you. GOOD NEWS! If you have made wrong choices, this means you have control and can move forward in life making right choices. It is never too late to start making right choices. But again, it is a choice. Begin to listen to what comes out of your mouth. What are you confessing over your life? What are you thinking about? Are you speaking life or death? Are you choosing life or death?

Isaiah 54:14-17 In righteousness you shall be established; you shall be far from oppression, for you shall not fear; and from terror, for it shall not come near you. Indeed they shall surely assemble, but not because of Me. Whoever assembles against you shall fall for your sake. "Behold, I have created the blacksmith who blows the coals in the fire, who brings forth an instrument for his work; and I have created the spoiler to destroy. No weapon formed against you shall prosper, and every tongue which rises against you in judgment you shall condemn. This is the heritage of the servants of the Lord, and their righteousness is from Me."

The Lord gave me this scripture a couple of years ago when a former employee placed a grievance against me with the Department of Workforce Development, reporting that I had unfairly terminated her based on her disease. This was not true, however, I was in a battle. The Lord gave me Isaiah 54:14-17 to stand on which gave me an immediate peace. Every time fear tried to move in on me, I read this scripture and fear would leave. I continued to stand on and confess this scripture until the day I was informed the case was found in my favor.

Wrongful accusations or diseases are examples of weapons formed against us. Accusations that rise against you can be likened to a negative doctors report which rises against you. These things shall not prosper when you put your trust in the Lord.

Fear can make the circumstance or problem seem bigger than God. Fear is a tactic from the enemy. It is not a "normal" response, it is a demonic response; it does not come from God. **2 Timothy 1:7 says, "For God has not given us a spirit of fear, but of power and of love and of a sound mind."** Notice God calls fear a spirit.

Christians should live a life of victory. We have a defeated enemy. The Lord says no weapon formed against us shall prosper. However, victory does take some effort on our part. The key is believing Jesus and what He says. If you never read your bible, the devil can deceive you. Get in the word and begin to practice or exercise your faith by trusting what God says. Each time you have a victory your faith gets stronger and your confidence in God grows.

Romans 8:5-7 For those who live according to the flesh set their minds on the things of the flesh, but those who live

according to the Spirit, the things of the Spirit. For to be carnally minded is death, but to be spiritually minded is life and peace. Because the carnal mind is enmity against God; for it is not subject to the law of God, nor indeed can be. So then, those who are in the flesh cannot please God.

Faith starts in the spiritual world, prayer brings it into the physical world. You can be saved and have a carnal mind, a mind that is actively opposed to God. To be spiritually minded is to think on the word of God and agree with what He tells us no matter what is happening around us. You cannot decide how things will turn out by following your five senses. God loves us unconditionally and ALWAYS wants the best for us. God cannot lie.

3 John 1:2 Beloved, I pray that you may prosper in all things and be in health, just as your soul prospers.

2 Corinthians 10:3-5 For though we walk in the flesh, we do not war according to the flesh. For the weapons of our warfare are not carnal but mighty in God for pulling down strongholds, casting down arguments and every high thing that exalts itself against the knowledge of God, bringing every thought into captivity to the obedience of Christ,

In our minds we can have certain views, attitudes or thoughts based on our experiences, circumstances, or what we have been taught. For example, you may have been told God no longer heals today or you may have been told as a child that you would never amount to anything. Words are powerful. Neither of these statements are true, but if you believe them and meditate on them, they can become a stronghold in your mind. These thoughts, imaginations and attitudes come in disagreement with

45

God's word. In order to overcome them, you need to find the truth in God's word and meditate on His word. Ask the Holy Spirit to show you the truth.

Thought (seed) + Dwelling on the thought (watering the seed) = Full grown thought (plant)

Thoughts and words are like "seeds" that take root if you think on them long enough. If you get a negative thought in your mind and cast it down because it does not line up with God's word, it cannot take root and grow. On the other hand, if you dwell on a negative thought, it can grow into anger, depression, unforgiveness, bitterness, fear, physical illness or death. As you think thoughts, pictures begin to form in your mind called imaginations. Imaginations can be good or bad. If you can only see yourself sick, you will not be well. The Lord says to meditate on good things. God's word tells us who we are. Begin to imagine or picture yourself healed. In the NLT bible, Romans 12:2 says to let God transform you into a new person by changing the way you think.

What types of seeds have been planted in your mind and life? What have you been imagining? Sometimes our garden needs weeding. Whatever you are watering (thinking on) will grow. Seeds can be good or bad. Weed out what doesn't belong. Plant God's word in your heart.

Luke 8:11-15, 18 Now the parable is this: The seed is the word of God. Those by the wayside are the ones who hear; then the devil comes and takes away the word out of their hearts, lest they should believe and be saved. But the ones on the rock are those who, when they hear, receive the word with joy; and these have no root, who believe for a while and in time of temptation fall away. Now the ones that fell among thorns are

those who, when they have heard, go out and are choked with cares, riches, and pleasures of life, and bring no fruit to maturity. But the ones that fell on the good ground are those who, having heard the word with a noble and good heart, keep it and bear fruit with patience. Therefore take heed how you hear. For whoever has, to him more will be given; and whoever does not have, even what he seems to have will be taken from him.

If you only have a head knowledge (no root) of what God's word says, you may start out believing, but when trouble comes, you will fall away.

Romans 12:2 Do not conform any longer to the pattern of this world, but be transformed by the renewing of your mind.

How do we transform or renew our minds? Read the bible and meditate on God's word until it becomes revelation to you. Knowing what the scripture says is not the same as believing it whole heartedly. Exchange your thoughts for God's thoughts. Say/confess what Christ says, not what the negative doctor's report says or what the world says. Believe in your heart what God says and refuse to believe what is contrary to His word. The belief has to be more than a head knowledge of Christ's word, it must be a heart knowledge. Confess God's promises over your situation. As you confess God's word, really begin to meditate *(contemplate or purpose in your mind)* on the word so it becomes alive to you and you have revelation of the word. Once you get a revelation, you are believing in your heart, then when you hear a negative word, you can be confident in Christ's truth and cast down the negative word spoken against you. Renewing your mind needs to be done continually.

One year the respiratory flu was very bad in our area and

47

everyone was talking about it. Being the Infection Control Nurse I had numerous meetings over it, I had received several emails from the CDC related to the flu and listened to teleconferences about it. We had several staff getting sick. All of the information we were being fed was negative. I was becoming carnally minded. I started feeling ill during the teleconference and left the room because I could not listen to anymore. I knew what God's word said but had been fed more of the negative reports than God's word for days and I could tell it was affecting me. I had not been renewing my mind. By the time I got home, I was really tired and had to lie down. The Lord instructed me to watch a healing DVD that I had. I have several on healing but He directed me to a specific teaching. I of course did the thing any spiritual person would do, I said, "Lord, I'm pretty tired, maybe tomorrow." The next morning I felt like I was dying so I did what any good nurse would do, I heavily medicated myself with cold medication and went back to bed. I know if I had renewed my mind as the Lord instructed, I could have avoided the whole thing. My advice, stay in the word continually renewing your mind and if God gives you a particular instruction, follow it. Don't let the symptoms be greater than God's word in your life.

Another time I was sitting at my desk getting ready to leave work when I began to feel sick. My throat was getting sore, I started sneezing, my head was stuffy, and I felt feverish. I was already getting thoughts that I had to call in sick the next day. The devil is subtle. It doesn't take long before negative thoughts can take over in your mind. I stopped those thoughts and declared I was well and was not receiving sickness. Then I heard the Lord tell me to drink more water (same thing my husband tells me). I started drinking a bottle of water, then a second bottle and drank the third bottle on the way home. By the time I finished the third bottle of water, all of my symptoms left my body. Drinking water seemed like a strange directive at the time, but it sure worked.

Some people experience miraculous healings at conferences or a church service but lose the healing after they go home. The truth is they are healed, but if they do not know in their hearts that they are healed, Satan can deceive them by placing symptoms upon their body to cause unbelief and then completely rob them of their healing. Just because we are experiencing symptoms, it doesn't mean we are not healed. The devil uses symptoms against us to cause doubt. Someone that knows the word of God can recognize the lie and cast it down. Someone who does not know God's word may fall to the lie, thinking, "Maybe I didn't get healed." That's all it takes, a word of doubt and the devil is back.

Scenario: Someone is believing for healing, praying, rebuking, calling the elders and anointing with oil, all the things Christians know to do. They have found healing in the word of God. Another visit to the doctor reveals that things are much worse and that person has been given a death sentence with 3 months to live. If that person receives into their heart the diagnosis and death sentence from the doctor, they will die. Proverbs 13:12 says that hope deferred makes the heart sick. If doubt moves in, their prayer of faith is cancelled out. But if that person has a revelation of what Christ did for them and continues to stand firm on God's word, casting down the words of the doctor that set themselves up against the knowledge of God, they will live. Our problem many times is that we believe the word of the doctors over God's word. It takes a continual renewing of the mind to be victorious.

(NIV)2 Corinthians 10:5 We demolish arguments and every pretension that sets itself up against the knowledge of God, and we take captive every thought to make it obedient to Christ.

Isaiah 55:8-9 "For My thoughts are not your thoughts, nor are your ways My ways," says the Lord. "For as the heavens are higher than the earth, so are My ways higher than your ways, and My thoughts than your thoughts."

Proverb 3:5-6 Trust in the Lord with all your heart, and lean not on your own understanding; in all your ways acknowledge Him, and He shall direct your paths.

We cannot continue think our own thoughts, believe negative reports, use our own reasoning and rationalization or follow our five senses, and expect that we will get well. We need to trust the Lord fully, believing Him and His word. God says in Hebrews 13:5 that He will never leave or forsake *(fail)* us. God loves us and is never glorified when we are sick or die early. Who's report are you going to believe?

How do you see yourself?

See yourself as Christ sees you, through the word of God. As Jesus is, so are we in this world. We are righteous because of Jesus. Don't forget who you are. If you see yourself sick and defeated, you won't be healed. Begin to see or imagine yourself whole and healthy so you can move into the reality of it. Begin to see yourself as loved, highly favored and blessed. I had started just thanking God out loud daily that He loved me, wanted good things for me and that I was blessed and highly favored and what a difference. You may not feel it or believe it at first but eventually you will and it makes a great difference how you look at things. If you know you are loved, blessed, and highly favored it sure can make your outlook on things change for the better. If you know that God is for you, no one can be against you. Meditate on God's love for you.

1 John 4:17 Love has been perfected among us in this: that we may have boldness in the day of judgment; because as He is, so are we in this world.

James 1:23-25 For if anyone is a hearer of the word and not a doer, he is like a man observing his natural face in a mirror; for he observes himself, goes away, and immediately forgets what kind of man he was. But he who looks into the perfect law of liberty and continues in it, and is not a forgetful hearer but a doer of the work, this one will be blessed in what he does.

The word of God is the mirror we are to see ourselves in. In order to see in the mirror, you must spend time in the word.

Jesus: The Baggage Handler

If you have a religious view of other people or yourself, you need to be set free in your thinking. Religion is not love. Jesus is love. If you are judgmental of others or believe you are more righteous than others, you are religious. If you are sin conscious or if you are pointing out others flaws and sins to them in a judgmental way, you are religious. If you feel guilty and condemned over your past, you have religious thinking.

Sin is not the problem. The bible says in 1 John 2:2 Jesus died for the sins of the whole world. The sin problem was taken care of by the blood of Jesus. The problem comes in when we reject the payment for our sins, the blood of Jesus. Jesus completely paid the price for our sins. We do not need to keep paying for them. When someone receives Jesus as their Lord and Savior, God says He remembers their sins no more. Jesus says we have become the righteousness of God. When God sees us, He sees us as He sees Jesus. It's because of what Jesus has done for us, not because of what we have done for Jesus or because of our righteousness. 1 John 4:17 As Jesus is, so are we in this world.

Romans 6:14 For sin shall not have dominion over you, for you are not under law but under grace.

When you operate under the law or religion, sin has dominion over you. You will always be sin conscious which brings guilt and condemnation. When you operate in God's grace, sin does not have dominion over you and therefore you experience the freedom of Christ.

Everyone has baggage in some form or another. Baggage can be feelings, circumstances, beliefs, bad habits, sins or addictions that hinder your freedom, progress and development. Emotional baggage can keep you from thinking clearly. Baggage is anything that hinders you from a victorious life. As you grow and mature in Christ, the baggage falls off automatically.

Pointing out others sins to them can have negative effects. If we start condemning Christians or other people that may not even know that they are in sin, they may turn from God. If people are feeling ashamed, guilty and unworthy, they may hide from God instead of running toward Him. People already know what is wrong with them, they need to know what can be right and that comes through the love of Christ. Remember, the bible says anything not done in faith (doubt) is sin, overeating is sin. In John 8:7, Jesus told the religious Pharisees, he who is without sin, cast the first stone. Remember that David was a murderer and an adulterer, but yet God called him a man after His own heart. How can that be? God does not see as man sees, He looks at our heart which reveals the real man. Looking righteous on the outside, doesn't mean you are righteous on the inside where it actually counts.

Little children act like little children, getting into trouble at times. Childlike behaviors diminish as people mature. As we grow or mature in Christ, the baggage falls off automatically. I am not saying that we shouldn't warn people in a loving manner if they are on a path to destruction, I'm saying, don't crush someone's spirit. The key is to do it in love. The Lord tells us to edify each other, not judge and condemn each other. **Matthew 7:1-3 "Judge not, that you not be judged. For with what judgment you judge, you will be judged; and with the measure you use, it will be measured back to you. And why do you look at the speck in your brother's eye, but do not consider the plank in your own eye?"**

The bible talks about infants in Christ and the mature. Just as we are born physically in the world as a baby and grow up, the same is true when you are born again, you must grow up. The problem is that many receive Christ and never grow up. They remain an infant tossed back and forth by every teaching they hear because they are not renewed in their mind. Many Christians have more carnal thinking than spiritual thinking because they do not know the word of God. Being an infant in Christ can lead to believing every teaching you hear. The problem is, not every teaching you hear is the truth. **1 Corinthians 3:1-3 And I, brethren, could not speak to you as spiritual people but as to carnal, as to babes in Christ. I fed you with milk and not with solid food; for until now you were not able to receive it, and even now you are still not able; for you are still carnal. For where there are envy, strife, and divisions among you, are you not carnal and behaving like mere men?** The bible says in

53

Hebrews 5:12-14 For though by this time you ought to be teachers, you need someone to teach you again the first principles of the oracles of God; and you have come to need milk and not solid food. For everyone who partakes only of milk is unskilled in the word of righteousness, for he is a babe. But solid food belongs to those who are of full age, that is, those who by reason of use have their senses exercised to discern both good and evil. Many Christians do not even know that they are the righteousness of God. This is a simple and foundational truth that you need to know in order to be victorious.

When I was a new believer, I went to a woman's bible study and was informed that I was not even a Christian because I was in sin. I cried all the way home. I told John that I wasn't a Christian. He asked me to get my bible out. He had me turn to Romans 10:9-10, then he asked me if I had confessed Jesus as my Lord and if I had believed in my heart? I said, "Yes." He said, "Then you are a Christian. You are in Christ." Then he told me to turn to **Romans 8:1** which says, **"There is therefore now no condemnation to those who are in Christ Jesus, who do not walk according to the flesh, but according to the Spirit."**

Romans 8:2 says, **"For the law of the Spirit of life in Christ Jesus has made me free from the law of sin and death."** Condemnation is to be guilty. I was no longer guilty because of Jesus sacrifice.

If you are speaking guilt and condemnation to others, or feel guilt and condemnation, you do not understand the love of Christ, you have religious thinking. When someone receives the gift of salvation from Christ, you are set free in every area of your life; this includes sins, guilt, sickness and disease, and addictions. When you receive Christ, your Spirit is made perfect; this does not mean that all of your baggage is gone overnight. Jesus is the one who changes us from the inside out. It is a process, just like growing from infancy to adulthood. If you are trying to change in your own efforts or are trying to get someone else to change by following the Ten Commandments or a bunch of church rules, you have religious thinking. The bible says we have fallen from grace if we try to follow the law to be righteous. **Galatians 5:4 You have become estranged from Christ, you who attempt to be justified by law; you have fallen from grace.** Galatians 5:4 in the NLT reads: For if you are trying to make yourselves right with God by keeping the law, you have been cut off from Christ! You have fallen away from God's grace. God's grace is amazing because we get it as a free gift, we do not have to work toward it. When this becomes revelation to you along with the love of God, you have no choice but to change for the better; sin, sickness and addictions have to leave.

It is the love and kindness of Christ that leads to repentance or change of thinking, not the law or rules and regulations. In fact, the law, rules and regulations burden people down. My husband says, "Jesus impresses, religion oppresses". The bible says the law was given in order that we might know we are sinners. After you receive Christ, you are no longer under the law, but under grace. **Galatians 3:24-26 Therefore the law was our tutor to bring us to Christ, that we might be justified by faith. But after faith has come, we are no longer under a tutor. For you are all sons of God through faith in Christ Jesus.**

Jesus will take care of your baggage, if you let Him. I am not for sin, I am against it. If you let Jesus work in you, He will set you free from sin. The Holy Spirit will teach you if you are willing.

Distorted Perceptions

Have you ever wondered why some people are healed and some are not? Why it looks like God heals some and not others? I have. My husband and I have prayed for people who have been healed and people who have died. When you pray for someone who is healed, it's awesome. But when you pray for someone you are believing to be healed and they die, it is discouraging. It can put a lot of questions into your mind along with doubt. I didn't understand why some were healed and some were not. I knew God heals but what was the catch when someone didn't get healed?

A few years ago, my sister Mandy asked me why everyone was not healed and why we got sick. I could not answer her question. This set me on the journey to find some answers and I started writing this book in 2009. I started the book with healing scriptures then I put it away for a couple of years, again because I had a lot of questions. I knew God healed but what were the conditions?

All people are going to die at some point, but I believe all too often, the devil takes people out before their appointed time. I also believe just because we are all going to die, it doesn't mean we have to die sick.

Our perception is very important. Feelings and experiences can lie to us. Example 1: I prayed for people who didn't get well. If this is my only experience and I am going by experience, then my conclusion is God doesn't heal.

Example 2: If I pray for people and some get healed and some do not, my conclusion could be that God heals some and not others. He plays favorites. I could conclude that God loves me more than someone else because He healed me of three things. This of course is ridiculous thinking and is not true.

You cannot rely on negative experiences to know God's will. Some people say, "Sometimes God heals, and sometimes He doesn't." God's will is to ALWAYS heal. Healing is available and we have to receive it just as we receive salvation. Just because salvation is available to all, doesn't mean all receive the free gift. People go to hell every day even with salvation being available. The same is true about healing, people remain sick or die even though healing is available to all.

You need to know that God has already provided for healing at the cross. It is a done deal. If you think you need to do something to get God to heal you, other than renew your mind and believe Him or if you think you may be among the few He doesn't want to heal, you will miss it. Jesus has already provided for our healing. Our faith, believing with our heart, is what brings the physical manifestation. What is your perception?

In Numbers 13 there are two perceptions/views of the same circumstance. **Numbers 13:25-33 And they returned from spying out the land after forty days. Now they departed and came back to Moses and Aaron and all the congregation of the children of Israel in the Wilderness of Paran, at Kadesh; they brought back word to them and to all the congregation, and showed them the fruit of the land. Then they told him, and said: "We went to the land where you sent us. It truly flows with milk and honey, and this is its fruit. Nevertheless the people who dwell in the land are strong; the cities are fortified and very large; moreover we saw the descendants of Anak there. The Amalekites dwell in the land of the South; the Hittites, the Jebusites, and the Amorites dwell in the** mountains; and the Canaanites dwell by the sea and along the banks of the Jordan." Then Caleb quieted the people before Moses, and said, "Let us go up at once and take possession, for we are well able to overcome it." But the men who had gone up with him said, "We are not able to go up against the people, for they are stronger than we." And they gave the children of Israel a bad report of the land which they had spied out, saying, "The land through which we have gone as spies is a land that devours its inhabitants, and all the people whom we saw in it are men of great stature. There we saw the giants (the descendants of Anak came from the giants); and we were like grasshoppers in our own sight, and so we were in their sight."

Caleb and Joshua spoke to the congregation in **Numbers 14:9** **"Only do not rebel against the Lord, nor fear the people of the land, for they are our bread; their protection has departed from them, and the Lord is with us. Do not fear them." And the congregation said to stone them with stones. Now the glory of the Lord appeared in the tabernacle of meeting before all the children of Israel.**

In Numbers **14:22-24 "because all these men who have seen My glory and the signs which I did in Egypt and in the wilderness, and have put Me to the test now these ten times, and have not heeded My voice, they certainly shall not see the land of which I swore to their fathers, nor shall any of those who rejected Me see it. But My servant Caleb, because he has a different spirit in him and has followed Me fully, I will bring into the land where he went, and his descendants shall inherit it."**

In one report the men saw themselves as grasshoppers going against giants. They already saw (imagined) and spoke their defeat. Terminal cancer can be likened to a giant. If the cancer is perceived to be bigger than God, this equals defeat. Some start out believing but when more negative reports come, maybe they're told they have just weeks to live, doubt can move in. If they receive the negative report and believe it in their heart, they will die. It is so important what we believe in our hearts. We must meditate on God's word so God's word is more alive than any giant we face. Don't let doubt and unbelief cancel out your prayer of faith.

Caleb and Joshua's report was quite different. They spied out the same land but saw it from the Lord's perspective. They believed the Lord. They still saw strong people in the land but said they were well able to overcome them. They reported a good land, the Lord is with us, do not fear the giants. If the cancer is perceived as a giant, but the person can see them self well and see the Lord is well able to overcome the cancer and they continue to believe in their heart without doubting, the victory comes.

Who's report are you going to believe?

Words are powerful

I have worked with dying patients and hospice nurses. I just want to say I have absolutely nothing against hospice nurses nor do I believe they are out to speak people to death, these are just some of the things that I have observed. Hospice nurses often make comments the patient will be dead in so many days and the patient dies. I have seen this over and over. I believe that many of the patients comatose or alert, hear the death prediction and receive it as truth, lose hope and die.

I have also seen where the hospice nurse made a prediction and the woman just wouldn't die. She always commented, "I'm not sick. What are you talking about?" And I know she did not believe she was sick. This woman improved rather than declined so she came off of hospice services. After a period of time, she went back on hospice. She went unresponsive at one point and again the hospice nurse predicted her death. At this time, the nurse's were taking turns sitting with her. When I sat with her, I was just talking to her about Jesus. All of a sudden she sat up and said, "What are you talking about? It sounds like you think I'm dying." Again she refused to die. It is what you believe in your heart. This woman kept refusing to die, but I believe all too often people refuse to live by giving in to the word of death.

The Lord says He sets life and death before us, choose life. It is a choice.

My husband had become very ill with heart problems. The symptoms had been going on for a couple of weeks. He wasn't able to sleep because his heart was racing, he started having chest pain one weekend and refused to go to be checked, he was turning grey and looked like he had aged 20 years in a matter of days. We were praying. I will say it is difficult to watch someone you love have terrible symptoms. He finally went to see his cardiologist who immediately hospitalized him. My husband began making plans for me and my daughter to go and live with my parents after he died. I had thoughts racing through my mind about what I would do if he died. When I was driving back to the hospital, the Lord brought back all kinds of promises he had spoken over my husband. Death was not one of them. I just began to speak life over my husband. When I got to the hospital, I asked my husband what he was thinking because it was important that he was not dwelling on death. I could pray all I wanted but his will mattered too. My husband told me he had already spoken with the Lord and he had chose life. While in the hospital my husband had to go through a few procedures. Being a nurse is not always the best thing because in order to believe the Lord I have to cast down medical knowledge that sets itself up against the knowledge of the Lord. I always ask my husband not to mention that I am a nurse because I either look like a heartless wife or a really ignorant nurse. When the doctors started reporting negative life threatening results to me, I just said, "ok" and politely smiled. In my heart I was not receiving anything as truth that did not line up with the word of God. I spoke to the test results and told them the Lord has the last word. The bible says to speak to your mountain. My husband's heart condition was a mountain.

After my husband's hospitalization he had a follow up appointment with his cardiologist. His cardiologist hugged him and said, "I thought you were going to die. You go and tell people someone was watching over you." When I spoke with my husband's primary physician, he said, "We all thought he was going to die." Thank God Jesus is greater than any life threatening illness. Every appointment since has shown he's better and better.

Another friend of ours was on hospice. Medically she was closer to death than life. The nurse would come and visit her and tell her she was dying. Harriet would call my husband and me to tell us she had bad news, she was dying. We would go and pray with her and she would be well until the next visit by the hospice nurse. At one point the hospice nurse actually stopped us and said she didn't understand what kept her going, medically she barely had a blood pressure and her labs were horrible and on and on. We asked her to quit telling Harriet she was dying. We would come in and speak life to her and hospice would come in and speak death over her. I remember once, my husband asked Harriet if she wanted to live or die and she said, "I want to live!" My husband responded, "Then live!" And she did. She was up entertaining friends the next day. This went on for months. One day her son moved her to a hospice house for respite care and she died in 3 days. I cannot prove this, but my guess, death was spoken to her.

What's coming out of your mouth? Do you need to zip your lip? The bible says we speak life and death with our tongues.

Proverbs 6:2 You are snared by the words of your mouth; you are taken by the words of your mouth.

Proverbs 18:21 Death and life are in the power of the tongue, and those who love it will eat its fruit.

Matthew 12:34 Brood of vipers! How can you, being evil, speak good things? For out of the abundance of the heart the mouth speaks.

Matthew 12:37 For by your words you will be justified, and by your words you will be condemned (unfavorable judgment)**.**

What is coming out of your mouth? What you speak most about is coming from the abundance of your heart. Your heart is your will and determines the course of your life. Pay close attention to what is coming out of your mouth. Are you speaking just words, words of faith or words of unbelief and doubt. If you are believing for healing, you cannot speak negative words over your situation or believe the negative report from the doctor and expect to be healed. You must get in agreement with God and meditate on and speak what His word says no matter what the circumstance looks like. We have a part to play in our healing, we need to believe God at His word. Believers are supposed to believe.

Proverbs 16:23-24 The heart of the wise teaches his mouth, and adds learning to his lips. Pleasant words are like a honeycomb, sweetness to the soul and health to the bones.

Listen to what God says in Proverbs 16, the HEART of the WISE, teaches his MOUTH.

Ephesians 4:29 Let no corrupt word proceed out of your mouth, but what is good for necessary edification, that it may impart grace to the hearers.

(NIV)Proverbs 10:19 When words are many, sin is not absent, but he who holds his tongue is wise.

(NIV)Proverbs 12:18 Reckless words pierce like a sword, but the tongue of the wise brings healing.

(NIV)Proverbs 15:2 The tongue of the wise commends knowledge, but the mouth of the fool gushes folly.

(NIV)Proverbs 15:4 The tongue that brings healing is a tree of life, but a deceitful tongue crushes the spirit.

Satan has a deceitful tongue. Don't listen to his lies.

(NIV)Proverbs 21:23 He who guards his mouth and his tongue keeps himself from calamity.

(NIV)Proverbs 18:21 The tongue has the power of life and death, and those who love it will eat its fruit.

James 1:26 If anyone among you thinks he is religious, and does not bridle his tongue but deceives his own heart, this one's religion is useless.

Prior to this in James, he speaks about being doers of the word and not hearers only. He also speaks about forgetting what type of person we are when we walk away from the word. Pay attention to what God's word says and do it. Control what comes out of your mouth (bridle your tongue). Do not deceive your own heart by forgetting what God's word says. We do not forget who we are when we read and meditate on God's word. You won't get your healing by confessing and believing a negative report from the doctor or discussing it with all of your friends. Maybe the fact is cancer showed up on your x-ray, but the truth is Jesus took your sickness at the cross.

Change your thoughts and words, change your life.

Truth (God's word) > Fact (Doctor's report)

CHAPTER 5

DO YOU HAVE A HEART CONDITION?

~

The condition of your heart is very important because it reveals your true nature and motivation. The heart of a person is the person, their understanding, their will, their soul. The heart stands for the man himself; all his thoughts, desires, words and actions from deep within him. Proverbs says the heart determines the course of your life.

1 Samuel 16:7 But the Lord said to Samuel, "Do not look at his appearance or at his physical stature, because I have refused him. For the Lord does not see as a man sees; for man looks at the outward appearance, but the Lord looks at the heart."

Hebrews 4:12 For the word of God is living and powerful, and sharper than any two-edged sword, piercing even to the division of soul and spirit, and of joints and marrow, and is a discerner of the thoughts and intents of the heart.

What are you thinking in your heart? What are the intents of your heart? God's word is a discerner of the thoughts and intents of the heart. In Isaiah 44:20 it talks about a deceived heart; in Romans 1:21 a foolish heart, in Ephesians 4:18 blindness of heart, in Hebrews 3:12 an evil unbelieving heart.

Proverbs 4:23 tells us to guard our hearts because the issues of life flow out of it. In the NLT translation it says, "Guard your heart above all else, for it determines the course of your life."

It's very important to guard your heart. As the scripture says, "For it determines the course of your life." Believers in Jesus can be spiritually blind in certain areas such as healing if they do not understand the word. It is an understanding with your heart.

Philippians 4:6-9 Be anxious for nothing, but in everything by prayer and supplication, with thanksgiving, let your requests be made known to God; and the peace of God, which surpasses all understanding, will guard your hearts and minds through Christ Jesus. Finally, brethren, whatever things are true, whatever things are noble, whatever things are just, whatever things are pure, whatever things are lovely, whatever things are of good report, if there is any virtue and if there is anything praiseworthy-meditate on these things.

Matthew 6:25, 27, 31-34 "Therefore I say to you, do not worry about your life, what you will eat or what you will drink; nor about your body, what you will put on. Is not life more than food and the body more than clothing?" "Which of you by worrying can add one cubit to his stature?" "Therefore do not worry, saying, 'What shall we eat?' or 'What shall we drink? or 'What shall we wear?' For after all these things the Gentiles seek. For your heavenly Father knows that you need all these things. But seek first the kingdom of God and His righteousness, and all these things shall be added to you. Therefore do not worry about tomorrow, for tomorrow will worry about its own things. Sufficient for the day is its own trouble."

1 Peter 5:7 casting all your care upon Him, for He cares for you.

John 14:1 "Let not your heart be troubled; you believe in God, believe also in Me."

Romans 8:6 For to be carnally minded is death, but to be spiritually minded is life and peace.

God's peace guards our hearts and He gives instructions to follow to keep His peace. God tells us to be anxious for nothing, to meditate on the good things, to worry about nothing, to seek His kingdom and His righteousness, to cast all your cares upon Him, to not let your heart be troubled, believe in God, and be spiritually minded. God knows your heart.

To guard your heart:

Submit to God and His word and His mighty power. **James 4:7-8 Therefore submit to God. Resist the devil and he will flee from you. Draw near to God and He will draw near to you. Cleanse your hands, you sinners; and purify your hearts, you double-minded.**

Be obedient to His word. Do what the word of God says. **James 1:22-25 But be doers of the word, and not hearers only, deceiving yourselves. For if anyone is a hearer of the word and not a doer, he is like a man observing his natural face in a mirror; for he observes himself, goes away, and immediately forgets what kind of man he was. But he who looks into the perfect law of liberty and continues in it, and is not a forgetful hearer but a doer of the work, this one will be blessed in what he does.**

Believe and have faith in Him. Believe in your heart, don't doubt. **Hebrews 10:22-23 let us draw near with a true heart in full assurance of faith, having our hearts sprinkled from an evil conscience and our bodies washed with pure water. Let us hold** fast the confession of our hope without wavering, for He who promised is faithful. **Hebrews 11:1 Now faith is the substance of things hoped for, the evidence of things not seen. Hebrews 11:6 But without faith it is impossible to please Him, for he who comes to God must believe that He is, and that He is a rewarder of those who diligently seek Him. Romans 14:23 But he who doubts is condemned if he eats, because he does not eat from faith; for whatever is not from faith is sin.**

Trust Him fully. Don't put your trust in man above your trust in God. **Proverbs 3:5 Trust in the Lord with all your heart, and lean not on your own understanding.**

Be thankful. If you are complaining and grumbling, you are not being thankful. **Colossians 3:17 Whatever you do in word or deed, do all in the name of the Lord Jesus, giving thanks to God the Father through Him.**

Take your thoughts captive. Get rid of the thoughts that are opposed to God's word. **2 Corinthians 10:5 casting down arguments and every high thing that exalts itself against the knowledge of God, bringing every thought into captivity to the obedience of Christ.**

Meditate on His word. Read and think upon God's word often. **Psalm 119:15-16 I will meditate on Your precepts, and contemplate Your ways. I will delight myself in Your statutes; I will not forget Your word.**

Think about what Jesus has already done for you. You are what you believe in your heart.

Proverbs 23:7 For as he thinks in his heart, so is he.

Watch what you are filling your spirit with, life (spiritual things) or death (carnal things). If you are frequently thinking and speaking about sickness and disease, your symptoms, depression, death and other negative thoughts, remember you are what you think in your heart. The more you think and speak negative thoughts, the more rooted they become and you begin to believe in your heart. It is so important to guard your heart, the Lord tells us to guard our hearts above all else.

Do not let a stronghold of unbelief, anger, bitterness, depression, fear, anxiety or unforgiveness take root in you. Fill yourself with spiritual truths by meditating on God's word and pulling down strongholds. Meditating on God's word will change your thinking. There are plenty of scriptures on healing to meditate on. If you can change your thinking, you can change your life. You do not have to do it alone though, in fact, God says you can't do it alone. **John 15:4-7 "Abide in Me, and I in you. As the branch cannot bear fruit of itself, unless it abides in the vine, neither can you, unless you abide in Me. I am the vine, you are the branches. He who abides in Me, and I in him, bears much fruit; for without Me you can do nothing. If anyone does not abide in Me, he is cast out as a branch and is withered; and they gather them and throw them into the fire, and they are burned. If you abide in Me, and My words abide in you, you will ask what you desire, and it shall be done for you."**

Jesus says ask and it shall be done for you.

Proverbs 3:1-8 My son, do not forget My law, but let your heart keep My commands; for length of days and long life and peace they will add to you. Let not mercy and truth forsake you; bind them around your neck, write them on the tablet of your heart, and so find favor and high esteem in the sight of God and man. Trust in the Lord with all your heart, and lean not on your own

understanding; in all your ways acknowledge Him, and He shall direct your paths. Do not be wise in your own eyes; fear the Lord and depart from evil. It will be health to your flesh, and strength to your bones.

Proverbs 4:4-5 He also taught me, and said to me; "Let your heart retain My words; keep My commands, and live. Get wisdom! Get understanding! Do not forget, nor turn away from the words of My mouth."

Proverbs 4:20-22 My son, give attention to My words; incline your ear to My sayings. Do not let them depart from your eyes; keep them in the midst of your heart; for they are life to those who find them, and health to all their flesh.

Proverbs 12:25 Anxiety in the heart of a man causes depression, but a good word makes it glad.

If you are anxious and living in fear, you are not in faith. You can know you are in faith when you agree with God and are at peace. God's peace really does pass our understanding, it's a spiritual peace.

Are you blind, deaf and dumb?

Acts 28:25-27 So when they did not agree among themselves, they departed after Paul said one word: "The Holy Spirit spoke rightly through Isaiah the prophet to our fathers, "saying, 'Go to this people and say: "Hearing you will hear, and shall not understand; and seeing you will see, and not perceive; for the hearts of the people have grown dull. Their ears are hard of hearing, and their eyes they have closed, lest they should see with their eyes and hear with their ears, lest they should understand with their hearts and turn, so that I could heal them."

70

Don't harden your heart to God's word. A hardened heart causes spiritual blindness. To apply the word of God to your situation, you must have heart knowledge, not head knowledge. You must be able to perceive God's truths with your heart, just as you believed in Jesus for salvation, a heart knowledge. If you never meditate on the word of God, your heart will be dull to His truths. If you eagerly seek God's truth on healing, you will find it. Pain, physical illness, feelings, symptoms are all real facts that Satan uses to distract us from the truth.

James 4:8 Draw near to God and He will draw near to you. Cleanse your hands, you sinners; and purify your hearts, you double-minded.

Doubters are double-minded. **James 1:6-8 But let him ask in faith, with no doubting, for he who doubts is like a wave of the sea driven and tossed by the wind. For let not that man suppose that he will receive anything from the Lord; he is a double-minded man, unstable in all his ways.**

Doubt and faith conflict with each other. Faith with doubt mixed in means you are double-minded; two-souled, your heart is split and wavering. You are not trusting God with all of your heart. In James he talks about a double-minded man should not expect anything from the Lord. If you are double-minded, you are not in faith like it says in **Hebrews 11:1 Now faith is the substance of things hoped for, the evidence of things not seen, Hebrews 11:6 But without faith it is impossible to please Him, for he who comes to God must believe that He is, and that He is a rewarder of those who diligently seek Him, and Hebrews 10:23 Let us hold fast the confession of our hope without wavering, for He who promised is faithful.**

Faith is to trust God with an unshakeable, confident belief in

God's truth that is not based on physical evidence. To doubt is to be in disbelief, lacking trust. Wavering between faith and doubt makes us double-minded.

Psalm 19:14 Let the words of my mouth and the meditation of my heart be acceptable in Your sight, O Lord, my strength and my redeemer.

Proverbs 14:30 A sound heart (at peace) **is life to the body, but envy is rottenness to the bones.**

Proverbs 15:13 A merry heart makes a cheerful countenance, but by sorrow of the heart the spirit is broken.

Proverbs 17:22 A merry heart does good, like medicine, but a broken spirit dries up the bones.

Proverbs 27:19 As in water face reflects face, so a man's heart reveals the man.

Proverbs 28:14 Happy is the man who is always reverent, but he who hardens his heart will fall into calamity.

Proverbs 28:26 He who trusts in his own heart is a fool, but whoever walks wisely will be delivered.

John 14:27 "Peace I leave with you, My peace I give to you; not as the world gives do I give to you. Let not your heart be troubled, neither let it be afraid.

Romans 10:8-10 But what does it say? "The word is near you, in your mouth and in your heart" (that is, the word of faith which we preach): that if you confess with your mouth the Lord Jesus and believe in your heart that God raised Him from the dead, you will be saved (sozo)**. For with the heart one believes unto righteousness, and with the mouth confession is made**

unto salvation.

Colossians 3:15 And let the peace of God rule in your hearts, to which also you were called in one body; and be thankful.

Do You Have A Hardened Heart?

Do you have a hardened heart toward healing? A hardened heart dulls a person's ability to perceive and understand God's truths because a hard heart is insensitive and difficult to penetrate. The hard heart is persistent in resisting God.

In Mark 8:17-18 Jesus lists symptoms of a hard heart: spiritually unable to perceive, understand, see, hear, or remember. If you have a hardened heart you will not be able to perceive spiritual things. You will be blind to spiritual truths. You can be blind toward healing.

Mark 6:52 For they had not understood about the loaves (had not gained any insight from the incident of the loaves), because their heart was hardened.

In the KJV, Mark 6:52 says they did not consider the loaves. The disciples were surprised at the miracle. If we are surprised or shocked at miracles or answered prayers, we have a hardened heart in that area. Whatever you consider, study or think upon, your heart becomes soft to and whatever you do not think upon you become hardened to. If you think upon God's healing word, your heart will soften toward healing. If you ponder or think upon your illness or the symptoms you are having, your heart will become soft to your physical illness.

1 John 3:21-24 Beloved, if our heart does not condemn us, we have confidence toward God. And whatever we ask we receive from Him, because we keep His commandments and do those

73

things which are pleasing in His sight. And this is His commandment: that we should believe on the name of His Son Jesus Christ and love one another, as He gave us commandment. Now he who keeps His commandments abides in Him, and He in him. And this we know that He abides in us, by the Spirit whom He has given us.

Your heart constitutes what you believe in your inmost being. Your heart is your understanding. Your heart determines who you are and the path your life takes. God looks at man through his heart. People can see miracles and hear about miracles, but not gain any insight from them because their hearts are hardened. If you are shocked or amazed by miracles, you have a hard heart in that area. Miracles are wonderful, but we should not be shocked that God performs them, that's who He is. You need to think about the miracles of Jesus, consider them, study them and ponder on them.

A hardened heart is not easily penetrated, but a softened heart is weakened so it can be penetrated. If you have a hardened heart toward healing, you will not see healing results. If your heart is softened toward your illness, you will remain sick.

To reverse the hardened heart, meditate on God's word and renew your mind by letting God change you by changing the way you think. Keep your confidence in God, not your illness. Your heart is a key to your healing.

You will be victorious if you can harden your heart toward worldly thinking, and soften your thinking toward the word of God.

CHAPTER 6

STUMBLING BLOCKS TO HEALING

~

God wants everyone well. That does not mean all will be well. God also wants everyone saved, none to perish, but people perish and go to hell daily.

2 Peter 3:9 The Lord is not slack concerning His promise, as some count slackness, but longsuffering toward us, not willing that any should perish but that all should come to repentance.

1 Timothy 2:4 who desires all men to be *saved* (sozo) and to come to the knowledge of the truth.

Lack of knowledge can lead to doubt

If you do not know that Jesus has already taken care of healing, you may miss it. If you think He still needs to do it or you need to do something to get Him to do it, this leaves room for doubt. The Lord has been a healer since the beginning. His character does not change. He is love and He is faithful.

Hosea 4:6 My people are destroyed for lack of knowledge.

Malachi 3:6 For I am the Lord, I do not change.

Hebrews 13:8 Jesus Christ is the same yesterday, today, and forever.

God's thoughts are higher than our thoughts. God's ways are not our ways. Jesus is no respecter of persons. What he does for one, He will do for all.

This may sound somewhat unloving but I am going to share anyway. I had a staff member at one time that did many strange things claiming it was how she was taught. Families had brought up concerns with the way she did certain procedures so I worked with her and reeducated her on the proper procedure. About a week later, the same complaints arose. All I could think was that this girl was an idiot. I find no pleasure in disciplining or terminating staff but for some reason, I found great satisfaction in terminating this particular girl. As I returned her file to the HR desk, I turned and began to walk away when I heard the Lord say, "Stacy, I love her just as much as I love you." That's when you feel like a real jerk. In her defense, I can say that she did have good qualities such as she was very caring and enjoyed working with people. She was not an idiot, she just was not in the right job. What the Lord said has really stuck with me. My point is that God loves all of us and is no respecter of person. If He provided salvation for one, He provided for all. The same with healing, if it's available to one, it's available to all. Just because someone may not believe in God's promises, it doesn't mean He is not faithful.

Romans 3:3-4 For what if some did not believe? Will there unbelief make the faithfulness of God without effect? Certainly not! Indeed, let God be true but every man a liar.

Proverbs 4:7 Wisdom is the principal thing; therefore get wisdom. And in all your getting, get understanding.

Unforgiveness: the poison we drink

Unforgiveness causes stress and certainly can make you sick in your physical body and in your mind. If you get hurt or offended by what someone says to you, you have choices. You can grumble and complain to everyone what that person did to you or you can forgive and move on. Hanging onto what someone else said or did to you, no matter how bad it was, affects you negatively. When you choose to hang onto an offense and not forgive, this opens the door for Satan to have free reign in your life.

Signs of unforgiveness:

*Replaying the betrayal over and over in your mind or repeatedly telling the betrayal to others

*Dwelling on the negative event or negative images

*Blaming others for our circumstance or problems

*Painful situation has become your identity

*Persistent anger

*Depression

*Bitterness

Unforgiveness affects the person refusing to forgive. It separates people, and allows envy and jealousy to seep in. You cannot control what others do and say to you, but you are responsible for your reactions to others. If you cannot or do not forgive, you do not know the love of Christ.

Unforgiveness causes stress which can lead to illness. Chronic stress from unforgiveness can lead to anxiety, depression, anger, hypertension, pain, insomnia, and abnormal immune function which can cause illnesses such as cancer.

My brother-in-law Lamont has taught me many things. Lamont had asked my husband and I if we could move in with him and help him out with the house and some financial troubles he was having. We prayed about it and felt as if the Lord gave the okay and we moved. It was a very small house for all of us, Lamont, my daughter, my son, my husband and me, not to mention the fact that Lamont drank heavily. It was okay for a short while, but then my husband and I began to get very angry at Lamont for many of his decisions. Lamont did not always make wise decisions. Let me give you a mild example; we had bees swarming in the umbrella of the patio table that my 3 year old daughter was sitting at. To take care of the bees, Lamont began wildly spraying caustic Easy Off oven cleaner everywhere, just an example.

One night Lamont was drunk and he and my husband were in the kitchen arguing over another "poor decision" Lamont made. You cannot rationalize with an angry drunk man. After the argument, my husband told me, "I heard a voice that said, "Just hit him in the head with the frying pan.'" It's a good thing my husband can discern between God's voice and the devil's. He did not hit Lamont.

Over time, the anger kept building and I began to have severe neck pain. My husband and I became so angry at Lamont that my husband got me up at 2 am to read scriptures on anger; imagine my delight. We knew our anger toward Lamont was wrong, but it was real. After reading the scriptures and refocusing; the anger subsided along with the neck pain. We continued to pray for Lamont and things went along fairly well for the most part until one day, my husband and I were in the car and he mentioned something that Lamont had done. I lost it. The severe neck pain was back instantly. I immediately recognized the pain and anger were directly related. I had to turn it all over to Jesus.

At this point, my husband and I decided to move, we went to tell Lamont and he said that he was moving because he had just come into some extra money and we should stay and take care of things. When we parted ways, I can honestly say the anger was gone and so was the pain.

Don't let anger, unforgiveness or stress take you over. Let it go, it's for your benefit.

Luke 6:37 "Judge not, and you shall not be judged. Condemn not, and you shall not be condemned. Forgive and you will be forgiven."

Ephesians 4:31-32 Let all bitterness, wrath, anger, clamor, and evil speaking be put away from you, with all malice. And be kind to one another, tenderhearted, forgiving one another, even as God in Christ forgave you.

Matthew 6:14-15 For if you forgive men their trespasses, your heavenly Father will also forgive you. But if you do not forgive men their trespasses, neither will your Father forgive your trespasses.

The Lord said we must forgive others, it is not optional. Many people have been deeply hurt by someone's words or actions. Unforgiveness cannot be justified by what someone else has done to you. You need to make the choice to forgive. When you forgive, you are not saying that what that person did was right, but you are releasing them to God and trusting Him to take care of the problem. Remember God said to cast all your cares upon Him for He cares for you.

2 Corinthians 2:5-11 But if anyone has caused a grief, he has not grieved me, but all of you to some extent-not to be too severe. This punishment which was inflicted by the majority is sufficient for such a man, so that, on the contrary, you ought rather to forgive and comfort him, lest perhaps such a one be swallowed up with too much sorrow. Therefore, I urge you to reaffirm your love to him. For to this end I also wrote, that I might put you to the test, whether you are obedient in all things. Now to whom you forgive anything, I also forgive. For if indeed I have forgiven anything, I have forgiven that one for your sakes in the presence of Christ, lest Satan should take advantage of us; for we are not ignorant of his devices.

Notice we should not be ignorant of Satan's devices. Unforgiveness leaves an inroad for Satan. Satan waits for us to open a door that he may enter your life. Don't let him in through unforgiveness. Satan is seeking someone whom he may devour. Remember, forgiveness is for your benefit.

1 Peter 5:6-9 Therefore humble yourselves under the mighty hand of God, that He may exalt you in due time, casting all your care upon Him, for He cares for you. Be sober, be vigilant; because your adversary the devil walks about like a roaring lion, seeking whom he may devour. Resist him, steadfast in the faith, knowing that the same sufferings are experienced by your brotherhood in the world.

One way you can resist the devil is to forgive others. Don't hang on to lifelong garbage.

Colossians 3:12-14 Therefore, as the elect of God, holy and beloved, put on tender mercies, kindness, humility, meekness, longsuffering; bearing with one another, and forgiving one another, if anyone has a complaint against another; even as Christ forgave you, so you also must do. But above all these things put on love, which is the bond of perfection.

Matthew 18:21-22 Then Peter came to Him and said, "Lord, how often shall my brother sin against me, and I forgive him? Up to seven times?" Jesus said to him, "I do not say to you, up to seven times, but up to seventy times seven."

James 1:22 But be doers of the word, and not hearers only, deceiving yourselves.

Do not deceive yourself by not forgiving others. The Lord commands we forgive as He forgave us. If we are in unforgiveness, we are not in love. Love keeps no record of wrongs. If we do not love, we do not know God. In 1 Corinthians 13, it says if we do not have love, we are nothing.

In 1 John 4:7-8 says that if we do not love, we do not know God. In Matthew 22, you are commanded to Love God and love your neighbor as yourself.

Unforgiveness is self-centered; the focus is all about what has been done to you. Remember Jesus forgives us no matter what we have done. Love yourself enough to forgive. It removes the burden stress from your body.

The Cure for Unforgiveness is Love

Ephesians 3:17-20 that Christ may dwell in your hearts through faith; that you, being rooted and grounded in love, may be able to comprehend with all the saints what is the width and length

81

and depth and height-to know the love of Christ which passes knowledge; that you may be filled with all the fullness of God. Now to Him who is able to do exceedingly abundantly above all that we ask or think, according to the power that works in us,

God's love, not our anger, changes the people around us. Ephesians 3:19 says we need a revelation of his love. Knowing God's love surpasses head knowledge. When you are under God's love, no problem compares. Keep your eyes on Jesus. Unconditional love is not limited by conditions. In other words, His love never changes or fails based on our actions and our love for others should never change based on how they treat us. No matter what they do. I have been verbally abused, physically beaten, sexually assaulted and have had attempts made on my life. None of these things give me the right to hold onto unforgiveness. Nor does anything that has happened to you give you the right to hold unforgiveness. We are to forgive others and love others right where they are at. The bible says to bless those who curse you and pray for those that spitefully use you. Remember God's ways are not our ways.

Sometimes, we need to forgive ourselves. I have had many negative experiences in life, which I am responsible for many of the negative outcomes because of poor choices. I have done many wrong things to others and have said many hurtful things to others. I have been married four times with three divorces behind me. I seem to be the common denominator in the divorce trend. I have forgiven myself and now have a wonderful husband. I don't let my past direct my future. I can tell you firsthand, forgiveness for yourself and others sets you free. When you forgive, it is life changing.

After you forgive, I can guarantee there are always more

circumstances and more people to forgive in the future. It's ongoing. When dealing with people, you can guarantee you will be let down, disappointed and you will have offenses come at you. Don't let the devil rob you of your peace and your time. Think about how much time can be wasted just by being angry at someone. If this happens, you have just been robbed by the devil. Readily forgive.

If you are mad at your parents, children, siblings, spouse, or someone else, get over it. Forgive. Don't waste your time in unforgiveness. Many times people may have wronged you, but many times the people that hurt you are doing the best they can. Hurting people hurt others. It is the love of God that changes people. God does not make us work for His love, and we shouldn't expect others to work for our love. Freely you have received, freely give.

Matthew 22:37-40 (GREATEST COMMANDMENT) **Jesus said to him, "You shall love the Lord your God with all your heart, with all your soul, and with all your mind. This is the first and greatest commandment. And the second is like it: 'You shall love your neighbor as yourself.' On these two commandments hang all the law of the prophets."**

1 Corinthians 13:1-8 Though I speak with the tongues of men and of angels, but have not love, I have become sounding brass or a clanging cymbal. And though I have the gift of prophecy, and understand all mysteries and all knowledge, and though I have all faith, so that I could remove mountains, but have not love, I am nothing. And though I bestow all my goods to feed the poor, and though I give my body to be burned, but have not love, it profits me nothing. Love suffers long (is patient) **and is kind; love does not envy; love does not parade itself** (boast), it is **not puffed up** (proud); **does not behave rudely, does not seek its own, is not provoked** (easily angered), **thinks no evil** (keeps no record of wrongs); **does not rejoice in iniquity** (evil), **but rejoices in the truth; bears all things** (always protects), **believes all things** (always trusts), **hopes all things** (always hopes), **endures all things** (always perseveres). **Love never fails.**

Galatians 5:6 For in Christ Jesus neither circumcision nor uncircumcision avails anything, but faith working through love.

After I was saved, if you would have asked me if I had forgiven my ex-husband, my answer would have been yes. After I sat in a room with him, it was evident the real answer was no. Apparently I had some deep seeded anger from ten years prior. I actually believe my anger was past the seed state and into a deeply rooted full grown tree. My oldest daughter was in counseling and we had a group session with my ex-husband, my son, my daughter and me. My ex-husband began to speak and brought up something from the past. Apparently it was not that important because I do not even remember what it was about. What I do remember is that I felt an anger rise from the pit of my stomach all the way to my face. My reaction could be more accurately described as a fit of a rage, not just anger. My left arm swung around with my index finger pointing straight at him as I said these words, "You! You have such a warped sense of reality!" My left arm swinging around in a circular motion as I pointed at him again and again like I was a professional pitcher. I continued to yell at him while I could hear a voice in my left ear saying, "Shut up Stacy. Shut up Stacy." I ignored the voice and just kept yelling at him. The counselor had clearly lost control of this session, her eyes were wide open, my daughter stood up and left the room crying. Soon after I stopped yelling, my son and my ex-husband left the room and went into the hall. I sat there still feeling somewhat angry when I heard the Lord say, "Now, go and tell him you forgive him." I politely replied, "No, I am not." Then I heard the Lord say again, "Now, go and tell him you forgive him." Again I resisted. The third time the Lord spoke, I got up, went into the hall where my ex-husband was and stated, "Scott, I have something to say." He replied, "I don't want to hear anything you have to say." I certainly didn't blame him after the "counseling session" we just had. Again I said, "I have something to say and I'm just going to say it. I forgive you for anything that happened while we were married and I hope you can forgive me for anything I did." At that moment I felt a physical heaviness lift from my shoulders. I felt it leave. I know that I definitely benefited from forgiving him. The Lord spoke to me once more about forgiveness stating, "If I couldn't truly love others, I couldn't earnestly pray for them." If I would have stayed in unforgiveness, I could not have truly prayed having my faith working through love. Not long ago my daughter called and said she heard words that she never thought would come out of her dad's mouth, "I'm going to bible study tonight." In addition to him going to bible study, he is remarried to a Christian woman. That's a praise the Lord.

1 Peter 4:8 And above all things have fervent love for one another, for "love will cover a multitude of sins."

Proverbs 10:12 Hatred stirs up strife, but love covers all sins.

1 Corinthians 13:13 And now abide faith, hope, love, these three; but the greatest of these is love.

1 Corinthians 14:1 Pursue love, and desire spiritual gifts, but especially that you may prophesy.

Matthew 5:44 But I say to you, love your enemies, bless those who curse you, do good to those who hate you, and pray for those who spitefully use you and persecute you.

1 John 2:9-11 He who says he is in the light, and hates his brother, is in darkness until now. He who loves his brother abides in the light, and there is no cause for stumbling in him. But he who hates his brother is in darkness and walks in darkness, and does not know where he is going, because the darkness has blinded his eyes.

1 John 4:7-8 Beloved, let us love one another, for love is of God; and everyone who loves is born of God and knows God. He who does not love does not know God, for God is love.

1 John 4:11-12 Beloved, if God so loved us, we also ought to love one another. No one has seen God at any time. If we love one another, God abides in us, and His love has been perfected in us.

1 John 4:18 There is no fear in love; but perfect love casts out fear, because fear involves torment. But he who fears has not been made perfect in love.

A few years ago my brother-in-law Lamont came to one of our bible studies brining his girlfriend Melanie that we had never met. We had been praying for him to come to bible study for some time and this was the night. My husband came to pick me up at work and had left Lamont and Melanie at the house. By the time we got home, we had about thirty minutes before the others would arrive. When we walked in, my heart dropped. There were beer cans all over the table and both Lamont and Melanie were drunk. Melanie could hardly walk or talk, I wasn't even able to understand her because her words were so slurred. Apparently she mixed her alcohol with her prescription drugs, not a good idea. I was trying to hide my feelings but I was upset to say the least, anger was mixed in with my feelings of embarrassment that I would have as soon as the other girls from work got there. Again, another opportunity for me to work on love for others. When the others arrived, we introduced everyone and sat down to dinner. Melanie's face was almost completely in her plate because she was barely coherent. As we began to speak about Jesus during dinner, Melanie sobered right before our eyes. She had absolutely no sign of impairment, her speech cleared, her eyes cleared, she became bright and joined the conversation. Jesus is AMAZING! Jesus loves us right where we're at, we should do the same.

Lamont and Melanie had left a little earlier than the rest. When they had gone, the rest of us looked at each other and said, "Did you see that?" It was dramatic. We all witnessed Melanie's instant sobering. Jesus loves all of us and He really wants us well in every area of our lives.

GOD'S KIND OF LOVE: Unconditional love is not based on our performance. God loves us for who we are, no matter what. God is love. We are to love others the way God loves us.

Fear, doubt and unbelief: Faith in Reverse

Unbelief will kill your faith. If we are in fear, we are not in faith. We don't need more faith, we need less doubt.

Luke 17:5-6 And the apostles said to the Lord, "Increase our faith." So the Lord said, "If you have faith as a mustard seed, you can say to this mulberry tree, 'Be pulled up by the roots and be planted in the sea,' and it would obey you."

Luke 8:50 But when Jesus heard it, He answered him, saying, "Do not be afraid; only believe, and she will be made well."

2 Timothy 1:7 For God has not given us a spirit of fear, but of power and of love and of a sound mind.

Fear is not a natural response to any circumstance, it is a demonic response. If fear was ok or normal, God's love wouldn't cast it out.

Job 3:25 For the thing I greatly feared has come upon me, and what I dreaded has happened to me.

1 John 4:18 There is no fear in love; but perfect love casts out fear, because fear involves torment. But he who fears has not been made perfect in love.

When you know how much God loves you, fear leaves. When you know how much God loves you, your faith abounds because you fully trust him. Ask God for a revelation of His love.

The Lord had told me to study love a while back. I was pretty sure I knew what love was, but I didn't really understand it or the importance of it. We need to understand love in order to receive what God has for us. It is a key to our faith working. The bible says to be rooted and grounded in love, it says our faith works through love, it says perfect love casts out fear. Where there is no fear, you have no doubt. When you know you are loved, you can love others right where they are at. When you know you are loved, you will know without a doubt that God wants the best for you.

Wrong teaching = Doubt

If you have been taught in church, never questioning anything the pastor says, you may have man's teaching and not God's. Some ministers have preached against healing in God's word causing unbelief and doubt. Perhaps you have heard teachings such as it is not always God's will to heal, God heals some and not others, God places sickness on us to teach lessons, you're in sin and that's why you are sick, or healing passed away with the apostles. If you have been taught wrong ideas and received it as truth, it will prevent you from receiving from God. Thinking intellectually from your mind or positive thinking does not produce healing. Once you have the revelation from God, believing in your heart produces healing.

You cannot rely on your church to teach you all things or in some cases, anything. First of all, you may not be receiving the truth; second, even if you are receiving the truth, you do not spend enough time in church to grow to maturity in Christ. You must search the scriptures for yourself asking the Holy Spirit to teach you. If you know the word of God for yourself, you will not be moved by every false teaching you hear. Pastors and ministers are human just like you. This may sound shocking, but some pastors do not even know Christ as their Savior, they may know religion, but not Christ. I am not suggesting you stop attending church or listening to your pastor, minister, or other teachers, I am saying, if you are in question about something or something just doesn't sit right with you, search the scriptures for yourself and ask the Holy Spirit for revelation. Don't take everything you hear as truth. If you search with all your heart, you will find the truth. In finding the truth, you have got to set all preconceived ideas aside.

When I first met the Lord, I asked other Christians the questions I had or watched pastors on T.V. instead of searching the scriptures for myself. Some things were right, and some were religious teachings. I was shaken up a lot, never having the confidence in God that I do today. Sometimes I questioned if I was even saved. If you are feeling condemned and guilty, you are most likely thinking religiously. I thought things like, do good to get good. My religious thinking held me back at times from praying for others because I did not feel worthy, maybe because I had not prayed enough or read enough. First of all, it's Christ who is answering the prayer, not me. Secondly, if we have to wait for people to be perfect, we will never get anything accomplished. Thank God for Jesus and all that He has done.

Many religions teach water baptism saves; some teach you need to get baptized as an infant, some as an adult. Recently, I met a woman that said she had always been worried about children dying without being baptized. She was concerned they would go to hell. She has spent her entire adult life without peace over this because she was taught that you must be baptized as an infant. In the bible, there is not one baby that is baptized; everyone baptized is old enough to make a decision. The bible teaches, Jesus saves, not baptism. **Acts 16:30-31 And he brought them out and said, "Sirs, what must I do to be saved? So they said, "Believe on the Lord Jesus Christ, and you will be saved, you and your household." Mark 16:16 "He who believes and is baptized will be saved; but he who does not believe will be condemned."** In Mark, if you read who is condemned, it is he who does not believe, not he who is not baptized. All through the scriptures, the bible speaks about believing unto the Lord Jesus and you will be saved. In Luke 23, the thief on the cross with Jesus, the thief who believed in Him, Jesus told him would be in Paradise with Him. The thief never had an opportunity to be baptized, but he did believe on the Lord Jesus. You have to make the decision, either baptism saves or it doesn't. It's not, sometimes it does, and sometimes it doesn't. I am not against baptism, I am for it because Jesus tells us to be baptized. I am saying that Jesus is the Savior. Your sins are covered because of the blood of Jesus. The bible says there is no remission of sins without the shedding of blood. It does not say without baptism. You can take an unsaved person and submerge them for baptism; this only produces a wet unsaved person. People in the bible get baptized after they believe. Children belong to the Lord Jesus up until the point they can make a decision for or against Christ. The idea that baptism saves is an example of a topic that has different religious teachings behind it. Many people believe baptism saves; but just because many people believe something, it doesn't make it the truth.

As long as we are talking about baptism, let's talk about baptism in the Holy Spirit. Some churches teach against the baptism in the Holy Spirit, some even teach it is a doctrine of the devil. The devil would love you to believe that. John and I had just moved and I had only worked with Sherry for a couple of months. We discussed Jesus frequently. She had a dream one night that she needed to be saved; she said Jesus kept telling her she must be saved. She came into work and asked me to pray with her and she received Jesus right there. We never had discussed speaking in tongues. One Monday morning, Sherry came into work and said she had heard the best sermon ever. She said the sermon was about speaking in tongues and how it was from the devil. This caught me off guard and I replied, "That's a lie from the pit of hell." I told her that I spoke in tongues and it certainly was not from the devil. God gives good gifts. I told Sherry that being baptized in the Holy Spirit empowers the believer. Now there was another woman, Lori, that worked with us. Lori and Sherry had been friends for a couple of years, and Lori was someone she trusted. Sherry was still in question about tongues, she had gone to Lori and told her what I had said. The beauty of it all; the Lord knows exactly who to send people to for confirmation. I did not know that Lori was baptized in the Holy Spirit. Sherry asked about speaking in tongues, Lori explained to her that it was a gift and that she had spoke in tongues for many years. The perfect set up by God.

I hope you are still with me because the baptism of the Holy Spirit is a gift that can benefit your spiritual life. The baptism of the Holy Spirit is of great importance. Acts 1:5 says that John baptized with water; but the apostles would be baptized with the Holy Spirit. Acts 1:8 says that they would receive power when the Holy Spirit came upon them; they would be powerful witnesses of Jesus. The baptism of the Holy Spirit empowers the believer. It was so important for the believers that Jesus commanded them not to leave Jerusalem until they received the Promise. Acts 2:4 says they were filled with the Holy Spirit and spoke with other tongues. Ephesians 5:18 says to be filled with the Spirit. When we first receive Jesus as Lord and Savior, when we believe unto Him, Ephesians 1:13 says we are sealed with the Holy Spirit. The baptism of the Holy Spirit is a separate gift and a necessary gift if you want to do the things Jesus did. In Mark 16:17 says that these signs will follow the believer: casting out demons, speaking in new tongues, take up serpents, drink poison without ill effect, lay hands on the sick and they will recover.

It is very important to receive the baptism of the Holy Spirit if you are going to lead a victorious life. This is why the devil fights against it, he knows the importance and he will do anything to keep Christians ineffective. Paul says in 1 Corinthians 14:5 that he wished all spoke in tongues and in verse 18 that he thanks God because he speaks in tongues more than everyone else. Some of the benefits of speaking in tongues are: speaking the word of God with boldness, building your faith, you can pray without ceasing when you do not know what to pray, pray the perfect will of God, speaking directly to God and edifying yourself. Read the following scriptures to see the benefits of being filled with the Holy Spirit.

Acts 4:31 And when they had prayed, the place where they were assembled together was shaken; and they were all filled with the Holy Spirit, and they spoke the word of God with boldness.

Jude 20 But you, beloved, building yourselves up on your most holy faith, praying in the Holy Spirit.

Ephesians 6:18 praying always with all prayer and supplication in the Spirit, being watchful to this end with all perseverance and supplication for all the saints-

Romans 8:26-27 Likewise the Spirit also helps in our weaknesses. For we do not know what we should pray for as we ought, but the Spirit Himself makes intercession for us with groaning which cannot be uttered. Now He who searches the hearts knows what the mind of the Spirit is, because He makes intercessions for the saints according to the will of God.

1Corinthians 14:2 For he who speaks in a tongue does not speak to men but to God, for no one understands him; however, in the spirit he speaks mysteries.

1 Corinthians 14:4 He who speaks in a tongue edifies himself, but he who prophesies edifies the church.

1 Corinthians 14:14 For if I pray in a tongue, my spirit prays, but my understanding is unfruitful.

A few years ago, I had a nurse working for me that was a Jehovah's Witness. She had told me that she could read any

93

bible, it didn't have to be the Jehovah Witness bible, The New World Translation. I found that interesting and wondered how she could be so misled if she could read any bible. Tammy had told me that when she joined the Jehovah's Witness church, she was taught what the scriptures meant. The Jehovah's Witness print the Awake and The Watchtower magazines, explaining the scriptures with their religious twist on things. The Lord showed me, that by having the scriptures interpreted for her by church leaders, she had preconceived ideas, an opinion forms before there is any evidence of truth. Each time the scripture is read, you remember and see what you were told the scripture meant and the lie takes hold deeper and deeper. Religious teachings can form strongholds in the mind. This is not only true for Jehovah's Witnesses, but it can be true for any religion or denomination not teaching the pure word of God. I would caution anyone that attends a church that has books and literature printed with their denomination's beliefs and discourages their members from reading anything else that is not from their denomination. If your religion says it is the only right religion and the only way to heaven, get out. Jesus is the only way, not religion. Read your bible, searching for the truth, asking the Holy Spirit to teach you.

Religion does not bring about the freedom that Christ does. Religious teachings bring bondage. Think about working toward your salvation, how would you know when you have done enough? Christ sets us free. Christ is exciting, He's alive. Religion turns people off while the love of Christ sets them free. **Galatians 5:1 Stand fast therefore in the liberty by which Christ has made us free, and do not be entangled again with a yoke of bondage.** Paul goes on to warn the people from falling back into religion by attempting to be justified by the law, thereby falling from grace. Paul says if we become enslaved again by the law, we become estranged from Christ. **Galatians 5:8-11 This persuasion does not come from Him who calls you. A little leaven leavens the whole lump. I have confidence in you, in the Lord, that you will have no other mind; but he who troubles you shall bear his judgment, whoever he is. And I, brethren, if I still preach circumcision, why do I still suffer persecution? Then the offense of the cross has ceased.**

In the NLT translation, Galatians 5:1-11 reads: So Christ has really set us free. Now make sure that you stay free, and don't get tied up again in slavery to the law. Listen! I, Paul, tell you this: If you are counting on circumcision to make you right with God, then Christ cannot help you. I'll say it again. If you are trying to find favor with God by being circumcised, you must obey all of the regulations in the whole law of Moses. For if you are trying to make yourselves right with God by keeping the law, you have been cut off from Christ! You have fallen away from God's grace. But we who live by the Spirit eagerly wait to receive everything promised to us who are right with God through faith. For when we place our faith in Christ Jesus, it makes no difference to God whether we are circumcised or not circumcised. What is important is faith expressing itself in love. You were getting along so well. Who has interfered with you to hold you back from following the truth? It certainly isn't God, for He is the one who called you to freedom. But it takes only one wrong person among you to infect all the others-a little yeast spreads quickly through the whole batch of dough! I am trusting the Lord to bring you back to believing as I do about these things. God will judge that person, whoever it is, who has been troubling and confusing you. Dear brothers and sisters, if I were still preaching that you must be circumcised-as some say I do-why would the Jews persecute me?

The fact that I am still being persecuted proves that I am still preaching salvation through the cross of Christ alone.

A little bit of wrong teaching can mess you up! Wrong teaching can prevent you from receiving from the Lord.

The bible says in **1 John 2:26-27 These things I have written to you concerning those who try to deceive you. But the anointing which you have received from Him abides in you, and you do not need that anyone teach you; but as the same anointing teaches you concerning all things, and is true, and is not a lie, and just as it has taught you, you will abide in Him. Galatians 1:11-12 But I make known to you, brethren, that the gospel which was preached by me is not according to man. For I neither received it from man, nor was I taught it, but it came through the revelation of Jesus Christ.**

Religion looks at our performance and proportions it to our answered prayers. I have heard it taught that sin prevents God from hearing you. That is a lie. The sin issue was resolved by the blood of Christ. He died for the sins of the whole world. I can remember one time that my husband had gotten sick. I said to him, "What sin are you doing that you keep getting sick?" As soon as I said it, I knew it wasn't right and I knew it wasn't from God. Thank God my husband can readily forgive.

If teachings such as, God places sickness on us to teach lessons, God heals some and not others, and God doesn't heal today are true; why do we run to the doctor to try and get well? What lesson can we possibly learn from sickness other than we want to be well? If you think it's a lesson you are to learn, don't go to the doctor, just suffer and get the whole lesson. If you think you may be one of the people God doesn't want to heal, don't pray or go to the doctor, stop fighting against God's will. This kind of thinking is silly. God does not teach us lessons by making us sick or holding healing back from someone. If that were true, we would have many wise people in the world with many lessons learned. God wants us well.

I will say, God has warned us not to do certain things (sins) because they are not good for us and can have negative consequences. Examples: Fornication can lead to sexually transmitted diseases. Stealing can lead to prison. You get the point. If God can't hear us when we are in sin, how can He help us with any of our problems, how can He help us get out of sin? If He can't hear sinners, this means we would have to do everything in our own effort, even save ourselves. How could we call on the name of the Lord and be saved if He can't hear us? It is not the righteous that need saving, it's the sinner.

Man's teachings and traditions can make God's word ineffective. If you are going to believe your pastor or religion over God's word, you will not see results. Just because a large number of people believe a certain teaching, it doesn't make it right. If it does not line up with God's word, it is not truth. Many times we are taught wrong from pastors we trust. I am not saying this wrong teaching is intentional, I'm just saying it makes God's word ineffective. Wrong teachings leave room for doubt.

Mark 7:13 "making the word of God of no effect through your tradition which you have handed down. And many such things you do."

True Christians have a personal relationship with Jesus Christ. Your trust is fully in Him for all you need. It is based on His goodness, not ours. We cannot do anything to earn His blessings, Christ did it for us. Grace is a free gift from God. We are no longer under grace if we are trying to follow the law or good works to get our blessing, healing or salvation. **Ephesians 2:8 For by grace you have been saved** (sozo) **through faith, and that not of yourselves; it is the gift of God.**

Galatians 5:4 You have become estranged from Christ, you who attempt to be justified by law; you have fallen from grace.

Religions are manmade and based on trying to get to God through rules, regulations and good works. Religion is based on people's efforts, being made right with God through their own efforts. If it is based on our goodness, then Christ died for nothing. A Christian's righteousness (right standing with God) comes trough faith in Jesus Christ. It is not Christ plus righteous acts or works.

If we are believing that we have to do something other than believe God for our healing, it will block healing. Sin doesn't block God's power, but trusting in our own efforts will. If God gives you a specific direction, obey it. Your healing is not based on your goodness, it's based on God's goodness. It's based on if we believe what He says without doubting.

Matthew 21:21-22 So Jesus answered and said to them, "Assuredly, I say to you, if you have faith and do not doubt, you will not only do what was done to the fig tree, but also if you say to this mountain, 'Be removed and be cast into the sea,' it will be done. And whatever things you ask in prayer, believing, you will receive."

Mark 11:22-26 So Jesus answered and said to them, "Have faith in God. For assuredly, I say to you, whoever says to this mountain, 'Be removed and be cast into the sea,' and does not doubt in his heart, but believes that those things he says will be done, he will have whatever he says. Therefore I say to you,

whatever things you ask when you pray, believe that you receive them, and you will have them. And whenever you stand praying, if you have anything against anyone, forgive him, that your Father in heaven may also forgive your trespasses."

Jesus did all he was going to do 2000 yrs ago. Jesus dealt with sin, the root problem of sickness and disease. How you view sickness is important. If you do not believe it is a part of the finished work of Christ then this view leaves room for doubt. Lack of knowledge, unforgiveness, fear, and wrong believing can all lead to unbelief, preventing a manifestation of healing.

Jesus could not heal many in His hometown because of unbelief.

Matthew 13:58 Now He did not do many mighty works there because of their unbelief.

Mark 6:5-6 Now He could do no mighty works there, except that He laid His hands on a few sick people and healed them.

Luke 8:50 But when Jesus heard it, He answered him, saying, "Do not be afraid; only believe, and she will be made well."

When Jesus said, "Only believe", he meant don't mix doubt with faith. ONLY BELIEVE!

Mark 9:17-29 Then one of the crowd answered and said, "Teacher, I brought you my son, who has a mute spirit. And whenever is seizes him, it throws him down; he foams at the mouth, gnashes his teeth, and becomes rigid. So I spoke to your disciples, that they should cast it out, but they could not." He answered him and said, "O faithless generation, how long shall I be with you? How long shall I bear with you? Bring him to Me." Then they brought him to Him. And when he saw Him,

immediately the spirit convulsed him, and he fell on the ground and wallowed, foaming at the mouth. So he asked his father, "How long has this been happening to him?" And he said, "From childhood. And often he has thrown him both into the fire and into the water to destroy him. But if You can do anything, have compassion on us and help us." Jesus said to him, "If you can believe, all things are possible to him who believes." Immediately the father of the child cried out and said with tears, "Lord, I believe; help my unbelief!" When Jesus saw that the people came running together, He rebuked the unclean spirit, saying to it: "Deaf and dumb spirit, I command you, come out of him and enter him no more!" Then the spirit cried out, convulsed him greatly, and came out of him. And he became as one dead, so that many said, "He is dead." But Jesus took him by the hand and lifted him up, and he arose. And when He had come into the house, His disciples asked Him privately, "Why could we not cast it out?" So He said to them, "This kind can come out by nothing but prayer and fasting."

The boy's father prayed, "Lord, I believe; help my unbelief." This tells me you can believe and have unbelief at the same time. Unbelief is the problem. When Jesus said, "This kind can come out by nothing but prayer and fasting." He was talking about unbelief. I believe the disciples looked at the circumstances. When they prayed, I'm sure the boy manifested the same things (spirit cried out, foamed at the mouth, convulsed him greatly) for the disciples as he did for Jesus. If the disciples prayed and saw the boy convulse and cry out, and they looked at the circumstances, this left room for unbelief. The bible says Satan comes like a roaring lion. Satan can roar pretty loud at times.

Definition of little faith: trusting too little, lacking confidence in Christ. I had a patient one time that had pain and swelling in his right arm. I asked him if he would like me to pray for him. He said, "Yes!" I prayed for him in faith and checked back with him the next day. To my surprise his arm was twice the size as the day before. I was shocked and overcome with embarrassment and unbelief. Faith left and doubt moved in. I said to him, "Those aren't the results I was looking for." He said, "Me either." We left it at that. I did not pray for him or offer to again. I was looking at the circumstances. He returned from his doctor's appointment that day with a diagnosis of pseudo gout. Pseudo means false. I believed a lie, I was deceived. Satan roared causing me unbelief.

My 9 year old son had pink eye in one eye. Medically speaking, pink eye is very contagious and takes antibiotic eye treatment to cure. We prayed and the next day his eyes looked much worse and both eyes were stuck shut. We told him to go wash his eyes, look in the mirror and command the pink eye to leave. He did and it left. His eyes were clear by the next day. Had we focused on the eyes looking worse, this would have left room for doubt. Two days later, we were at my oldest daughters house by my grandchildren. My youngest daughter got pink eye. By this time I was angry at pink eye. I took my daughter into the bathroom and I loudly commanded the pink eye to leave in the name of Jesus, and it left. This is an example of taking my authority and speaking to my mountain. My oldest daughter told me to keep it down, she had neighbors. You cannot be worried about what others think. Now at this point, you may be thinking, "Are you sure it was pink eye?" Yes. My grandchildren got the pink eye after we left and were given antibiotic eye drops from the doctor.

One of my patients asked to have me come to her room. When I entered her room she was crying and asked me if I could speak at her funeral. She had an appointment the next day for surgery for an infected tooth and with all of her other complications, she was sure she would die. I asked her if she wanted to die and her answer was, "No!" I then asked if she would like me to pray for her and she said, "Yes!" I commanded infection and pain to leave her body, I commanded the depression to leave her and spoke healing into her body. When I got done praying, she looked at me and said, "Wow, I feel great! I feel different. My pain is almost gone. I didn't think anything would happen." Because she said that she still had just a little bit of pain left in her jaw, I offered to pray again and get rid of the rest of the pain. She said, "Oh, no. This is good enough." I believe the rest of the pain would have left if we prayed again, but she settled for what she got.

Sometimes, the person you are praying for doesn't know the promises of God, but they can see that you believe and it can give them faith. I have asked people what they are believing will happen when they pray and have found some people expect nothing to happen when they pray. Why pray? If you expect nothing, you very well may get nothing.

Believe the promises of God. He is faithful. I have heard people speak against the "faith believers". This has always baffled me because without faith it is impossible to please God. My other thought is, if these faith believers are seeing results of healing and you are not, maybe there's something to this faith believing stuff. Anything you do not believe or respect, you will not participate in. If you are against it, how can you expect to receive it? Learn the word of God for yourself and start seeing results.

God is a Good God

You must settle in your heart that God is a good God and wants the best for you!

3 John 2 Beloved, I pray that you may prosper in all things and be in health, just as your soul prospers.

We are body, soul and spirit. When you receive Jesus as your Lord and Savior, your spirit becomes perfect and is sealed with the Holy Spirit (Ephesians 1:13); you are on your way to heaven. The physical body can present with symptoms of sickness or be in health. Your soul is your mind, will and emotions; basically how you think or believe in your heart. The condition of your soul will affect the physical body and the direction of your life. The more revelation you receive from the word of God, the more you prosper. When your soul is prospering, you will thrive in every area of your life.

1 Thessalonians 5:23 Now may the God of peace Himself sanctify you completely; and may your whole spirit, soul, and body be preserved blameless at the coming of our Lord Jesus Christ.

Being three part beings, we have a couple different scenarios that can happen. #1: If our soul (our will) lines up or identifies with our spirit, we will be well. When the spirit and soul agree, the body aligns automatically. This means that our thinking and our heart agree with the word of God. #2 If our soul (our will) lines up or identifies with our physical body which has symptoms of disease, we will remain sick. We are still saved but not prospering, we are loved but not enjoying the full benefits of Christ. It is extremely important we get our thinking to line up with God's word so we can prosper in all areas of our life.

2 Corinthians 1:20 For all the promises of God in Him are yes, and in Him Amen, to the glory of God through us.

2 Peter 1:2-4 Grace and peace be multiplied to you in the knowledge of God and of Jesus our Lord, as His divine power has given to us all things that pertain to life and godliness, through the knowledge of Him who called us by His glory and virtue, by which have been given to us exceedingly great and precious promises, that through these you may be partakers of the divine nature, having escaped the corruption that is in the world through lust.

John 15:7 "If you abide in Me, and My words abide in you, you will ask what you desire, and it shall be done for you."

Abiding in God's word means to stay, remain or continue in it. Stay in the word. Some prayers are answered immediately, seemingly without much effort, while other answers to prayers may take diligent time in the word, meditating on the word. The Lord says He is a rewarder of those who diligently seek Him. If you want the reward, you need to do more than go to church on Sunday and get prayed for here and there. Study and meditate on the word of God, renewing your mind. How badly do you want to be well? How much effort are you willing to put in to get the revelation from God?

Colossians 2:1-8 For I want you to know what a great conflict I have for you and those in Laodicea, and for as many as have not seen my face in the flesh, that their hearts maybe encouraged, being knit together in love, and attaining to all the riches of the full assurance of understanding, to the knowledge of the mystery of God, both of the Father and of Christ, in whom are hidden all the treasures of wisdom and knowledge. Now this I say lest anyone should deceive you with persuasive words. For though I am absent in the flesh, yet I am with you in spirit, rejoicing to see your good order and steadfastness of your faith in Christ. As you therefore have received Christ Jesus the Lord, so walk in Him, rooted and built up in Him and established in the faith, as you have been taught, abounding in it with thanksgiving. Beware lest anyone cheat you through philosophy and empty deceit, according to the tradition of men, according to the basic principles of the world, and not according to Christ.

Don't believe every teaching you hear, search the scriptures out for yourself and ask the Holy Spirit to reveal the truth to you. If you remain skeptical of God's word about healing, you'll miss it. *You don't get healed because you have intellectual knowledge, you get healed when you have revelation knowledge.* My editor says the previous sentence sums it all up; it is the best line in the book. She said if you missed it, reread it until you get it.

John 8:31-32 Then Jesus said to those Jews who believed Him, "If you abide in My word, you are My disciples indeed. And you shall know the truth, and the truth shall make you free."

John 8:36 Therefore if the Son makes you free, you shall be free indeed.

Abide in God's word and yield to His power. As you submit to God's word, you are set free. To accomplish God's will, we have to do our part. We must believe and cooperate with what God says. If you do not know it is God's will for you to be healed, this leaves room for doubt and unbelief. The root of fear and unbelief is lack of understanding how much God really loves us. If we knew how much God really loves us, we would not have any doubt when we pray. Start asking God for a revelation of His unconditional love. **1 John 4:18 There is no fear in love; but** perfect love casts out fear because fear has torment. He who fears is not made perfect in love.

Where have you placed your faith, God or man?

2 Chronicles 16:7-9 And at that time Hanani the seer came to Asa king of Judah, and said to him: "Because you have relied on the king of Syria, and have not relied on the Lord your God, therefore the army of the king of Syria has escaped from your hand. Were the Ethiopians and the Lubim not a huge army with very many chariots and horsemen? Yet, because you relied on the Lord, He delivered them into your hand. For the eyes of the Lord run to and fro throughout the whole earth, to show Himself strong on behalf of those whose heart is loyal to Him. In this you have done foolishly; therefore from now on you shall have wars."

2 Chronicles 16: 12-13 And in the thirty-ninth year of his reign, Asa became diseased in his feet, and his malady was severe; yet in his disease he did not seek the Lord, but the physicians. So Asa rested with his fathers; he died in the forty-first year of his reign.

In 2 Chronicles, the scriptures contrast trusting in God verses trusting in man. I am not suggesting to eliminate your doctor. I am saying, if you trust a negative doctor's report that says you are terminal over trusting what God says, that by His stripes you are healed, you may die.

If we continue to allow God to work in and through us, we will have victory. We must put our full trust in Him, believing His word. Don't have more faith in the negative report than faith in the word of God. America is very blessed, we have insurance and Medicare, wonderful medical doctors and many different

106

specialists. Again, I am not opposed to them, but what do you do when the medical system runs out of answers and hope for you? What YOU believe and who you put your trust in, matters!

CHAPTER 7

OUR FAITH

~

1 John 5:4 For whatever is born of God overcomes the world. And this is the victory that overcomes the world-our faith.

Jude 20-21 But you, beloved, building yourselves up on your most holy faith, praying in the Holy Spirit, keep yourselves in the love of God, looking for the mercy of our Lord Jesus Christ unto eternal life.

2 Corinthians 5:7 For we walk by faith, not by sight.

Faith always has a good report. If you are talking about all of the negative reports or symptoms, you are not speaking encouraging, faith words. Jesus has done it all and He says to rest in him.

Matthew 11:28-30 "Come to me, all you who labor and are heavy laden, and I will give you rest. Take My yoke upon you and learn from Me, for I am gentle and lowly in heart, and you will find rest for your souls. For My yoke is easy and My burden is light.

I had a dream a while back about a man in a wheelchair. He was paralyzed. His head and arms were strapped to the wheelchair to support him. Jesus walked into the room and all of the straps broke loose and the man was instantly healed. Jesus said, "Stop trying to carry the burdens I have already carried."

Be fully convinced or persuaded that God has done all that He has promised, not looking at your circumstances. In other words, do not consider your symptoms, illness, or the negative doctor's report. Remember, whatever you consider or ponder in your heart, your heart becomes soft to and whatever you do not consider, your heart becomes hardened to. Abraham did not consider his own body.

Romans 4:19-22 And not being weak in faith, he did not consider his own body, already dead (since he was about a hundred years old), and the deadness of Sarah's womb. He did not waver at the promise of God through unbelief, but was strengthened in faith, giving glory to God, and being fully convinced that what He had promised He was also able to perform. And therefore "it was accounted to him for righteousness."

Abraham did not look at the circumstances that were against him. He did not waver in his faith. His faith was accounted as right standing with God.

Matthew 7:7-8 Ask, and it will be given to you; seek, and you will find; knock, and it will be opened to you. For everyone who asks receives, and he who seeks finds, and to him who knocks it will be opened.

Matthew 18:19-20 Again I say to you that if two of you agree on earth concerning anything that they ask, it will be done for them by My Father in heaven. For where two or three are gathered together in My name, I am there in the midst of them.

Remember to look for people to agree with you in faith, not pity you. Having pity for someone never gets them healed or their prayers answered. If it's a terminal illness and you only pity the person and they are in agreement, they will likely die. Pity is not faith. The bible says where two agree, it will be done for them. Agree for healing.

Matthew 21:21-22 So Jesus answered and said to them, "Assuredly, I say to you, if you have faith and do not doubt, you will not only do what was done to the fig tree, but also if you say to this mountain, 'Be removed and be cast into the sea,' it will be done. And whatever things you ask in prayer, believing, you will receive."

Jesus said to believe and we will receive. He didn't say we might receive, He said we will.

Mark 11:22-24 So Jesus answered and said to them, "Have faith in God. For assuredly, I say to you, whoever says to this mountain, 'Be removed and be cast into the sea,' and does not doubt in his heart, but believes that those things he says will be done, he will have whatever he says. Therefore I say to you, whatever things you ask when you pray, believe that you receive them."

Jesus says to have faith in God. He also says to speak to the mountain. The mountain can be whatever you are facing, any kind of sickness or disease.

John 14:13-14 And whatever you ask in My name, that I will do, that the Father may be glorified in the Son. If you ask anything in My name, I will do it.

James 5:15-16 And the prayer of faith will save the sick, and the Lord will raise him up. And if he has committed sins, he will be forgiven. Confess your trespasses to one another, and pray

for one another, that you may be healed. The effective, fervent prayer of a righteous man avails much.

In James it says the prayers of a righteous man avails much or in other words, it results in a benefit. If you are in Christ, you are righteous. Have confidence when you pray for others or yourself.

James 1:5-8 If any of you lacks wisdom, let him ask of God, who gives to all liberally and without reproach, and it will be given to him. But let him ask in faith, with no doubting, for he who doubts is like a wave of the sea driven and tossed by the wind. For let not that man suppose that he will receive anything from the Lord; he is a double-minded man, unstable in all his ways.

The key is to believe without doubting. If you have questions, ask for wisdom.

Hebrews 10:23 Let us hold fast the confession of our hope without wavering, for He who promised is faithful.

Hebrews 11:1 Now faith is the substance of things hoped for, the evidence of things not seen.

Just because we do not see physical manifestations of healings immediately, it does not mean that it is not done. Faith is the substance of things hoped for, the evidence of things not seen. That's faith.

Hebrews 11:6 But without faith it is impossible to please Him, for he who comes to God must believe that He is, and that He is a rewarder of those who diligently seek Him.

Are you diligently, in constant effort, seeking Him? If you truly are, you will see your healing. Too often, I believe people start out in faith for their healing, but as time passes, doubt moves in because physical symptoms are still present. Diligently seeking is to be constantly seeking truth by renewing our mind.

A friend of ours was healed from Multiple Sclerosis. She gives her testimony all over the world now. She told me that the Lord had her teaching others about healing before she had the full manifestation of her healing. Her healing was not instant, but came as she taught others.

Romans 10:17 So then faith comes by hearing, and hearing by the word of God.

Matthew 6:9-13 "In this manner, therefore, pray: Our Father in heaven, hallowed be Your name. Your kingdom come. Your will be done on earth as it is in heaven. Give us this day our daily bread. And forgive us our debts, as we forgive our debtors. And do not lead us into temptation, but deliver us from the evil one. For Yours is the kingdom and the power and the glory forever. Amen."

Jesus told us to pray in this manner. If you look at this prayer, it says, "Your will be done on earth as it is in heaven." Think about it, there is no sickness in heaven. His will is that we are well. Religion has turned this prayer into vain or fruitless repetitions.

Ephesians 1:17-21 that the God of our Lord Jesus Christ, the Father of glory, may give to you the spirit of wisdom and revelation in the knowledge of Him, the eyes of your understanding being enlightened; that you may know what is the hope of His calling, what are the riches of the glory of His inheritance in the saints, and what is the exceeding greatness of His power toward us who believe, according to the working of His mighty power which He worked in Christ when He raised

Him from the dead and seated Him at His right hand in the heavenly places, far above all principality and power and might and dominion, and every name that is named, not only in this age but also in that which is to come.

Pray for the spirit of wisdom and revelation so your eyes can be opened to the exceeding greatness of His power toward us who believe. Living on the inside of us we have the same power that raised Christ from the dead. That power is more than enough to take care of any terminal illness, missing limbs or organs, dead people, financial problem or whatever is at hand.

We went to a church service with some friends, one of our friends didn't believe in healing because he was taught against it and another had a special built up shoe and used a cane to walk because her legs were not equal in length. When she was prayed for, her leg grew out about three inches, to an equal length of the other leg. This happened right before our eyes. After her leg grew, she no longer needed her cane to get around or the special shoes. Laurence, the former unbeliever in healing, became a firm believer in healing.

My husband and I have seen people healed of various diseases and raised from the dead. The Holy Spirit has had us intervene in people's lives only to find out later that they were going to commit suicide. We have had friends healed from COPD, cancer, fibromyalgia, MS and depression. We command pain to leave, and it leaves instantly. These are just some of the things we have prayed for or witnessed. If you are in awe or unbelief over any of these statements, you have a hardened heart toward healing. God says with Him all things are possible for those who believe. He also said He can do more than we can think or imagine.

In 2007, my brother-in-law called us to come over because my father-in-law was dying. Lamont was outside on the porch crying when we pulled up to the house because my father-in-law had already passed away. My husband commanded the death spirit to leave and called my father-in-law back from the dead. It took a few minutes before my father-in-law opened his eyes and responded. He was an eerie, glowing, white color, as if all of the blood was gone from him. Within 2 hours his color had returned and he was completely fine. He began to tell us that he knew before he died that he was dying and that it wouldn't be long.

As Christians, we have power and authority to raise the dead. The bible says we have the same power that raised Christ from the dead living on the inside of us. That's a lot of power. Jesus has given us His authority on earth. In order to get miraculous results, you have to believe what the bible says and act on it. You cannot think like the rest of the world. The bible says we are in the world, but not of the world.

(NLT) Romans 12:2 Don't copy the behavior and customs of this world, but let God transform you into a new person by changing the way you think. Then you will learn to know God's will for you, which is good and pleasing and perfect. Notice the bible says to let God transform you by changing the way you think, not the way you act. As your thinking is transformed, you learn the good and perfect will of God.

1 John 5:14-15 Now this is the confidence that we have in Him, that if we ask anything according to His will, He hears us. And if we know that He hears us, whatever we ask, we know that we have the petitions that we have asked of Him.

Romans 1:17 For in it the righteousness of God is revealed from faith to faith; as it is written, "The just shall live by faith."

Matthew 19:26 But Jesus looked at them and said to them, "With men this is impossible, but with God all things are possible."

Sometimes we may run into a brick wall counting on man because certain things are impossible for man. But with God, the tables turn in our favor. ALL is a big word and All things are possible with God. Nothing is impossible.

CHAPTER 8

HEALING SCRIPTURES

~

Matthew 4:23 And Jesus went about all Galilee, teaching in their synagogues, preaching the gospel of the kingdom, and healing all kinds of sickness and all kinds of disease among the people.

Matthew 9:35 Then Jesus went about all the cities and villages, teaching in their synagogues and preaching the gospel of the kingdom, and healing every sickness and every disease among the people.

Matthew 12:15 But when Jesus knew it, He withdrew from there. And great multitudes followed Him, and He healed them all.

Acts 5:16 Also a multitude gathered from the surrounding cities to Jerusalem, bringing sick people and those who were tormented by unclean spirits, and they were all healed.

Matthew 14:14 And when Jesus went out He saw a great multitude; and He was moved with compassion for them, and healed their sick.

Matthew 14: 35-36 And when the men of that place recognized Him, they sent out into all that surrounding region, brought to Him all who were sick, and begged Him that they might only touch the hem of His garment. And as many as touched it were made perfectly well.

Mark 6:56 Wherever He entered, in villages, cities, or the countryside, they laid the sick in the marketplaces, and begged Him that they might just touch the hem of His garment. And as many as touched Him were made well.

Luke 5:15 However, the report went around concerning Him all the more; and great multitudes came together to hear, and to be healed by Him of their infirmities.

Luke 6:18-19 as well as those who were tormented with unclean spirits. And they were healed. And the whole multitude sought to touch Him, for power went out from Him and healed them all.

Luke 9:6 So they departed and went through the towns, preaching the gospel and healing everywhere.

Luke 9:11 But when the multitudes knew it, they followed Him; and He received them and spoke to them about the kingdom of God, and healed those who had need of healing.

Jesus never denied healing to anyone.

Chapter 9

CONCLUSION

~

Acts 10:38 how God anointed Jesus of Nazareth with the Holy Spirit and with power. He went about doing good and healing all who were oppressed by the devil, for God was with Him.

Notice it is the devil who oppresses people with sickness. Some people get all funny when they think about casting out devils. Just know that if you prayed for someone and they got healed, a devil left.

Jeremiah 29:11-14 For I know the plans I have for you, declares the Lord, plans to prosper you and not to harm you, plans to give you hope and a future.

God has good plans for us.

John 16:33 "These things I have spoken you, that in Me you may have peace. In the world you will have tribulation; but be of good cheer; I have overcome the world."

Jesus has overcome the world.

John 16:23-24 "And in that day you will ask Me nothing. Most assuredly, I say to you, whatever you ask the Father in My name He will give you. Until now you have asked nothing in My name. Ask, and you will receive, that your joy may be full."

The word of God is a spiritual book and is 100% truth. When you receive Christ as Lord and Savior, your spiritual eyes are opened. You can then begin to ask the Holy Spirit to show you the truths of God's word. Without the Spirit, the bible is a dead book. The bible cannot be interpreted properly by those with intellectual knowledge, it has to be done through the Spirit. Get rid of all religious teachings that do not line up with the word of God and get filled with the Holy Spirit.

When you know the truth for yourself, you can be set free. In Philippians 2:9 it says that the name of Jesus is above every name, this includes the name of any illness, fear, depression, or whatever problem you are facing. Jesus is greater than ANY problem.

James 4:7 Therefore submit to God. Resist the devil and he will flee from you.

The first instruction is to submit or yield to God's power.

The second instruction is to resist or stand firm against the devil so he has no choice but to flee from you.

Often, I believe, we assist the devil instead or resisting him. For instance, we grumble and complain, we talk about how big our circumstances are instead of how big our God is; we get into fear and unbelief and are completely open to whatever the devil has for us.

The only authority the devil has over us, is the authority that we give him. Fear invites the devil.

We must get to the point that we know without a doubt that bad things are from the devil and good things are from God. Jesus is love and comes to bring us abundant life. The devil's purpose is to rob, kill and destroy. If your circumstance does not fit into abundant life, resist the devil.

James 1:16-17 Do not be deceived, my beloved brethren. Every good gift and every perfect gift is from above, and comes down from the Father of lights, with whom there is no variation or shadow of turning.

Remember everyone can be healed but not everyone will be. It is the same way with salvation, everyone can be saved but not everyone will. It is a choice. Your will is involved. To be successful you need to study and meditate on the scriptures until revelation comes.

You could never convince me that Jesus is not faithful. If you believe God picks and chooses who is and isn't healed, who gets their prayers answered, that is exactly what you are saying. If you believe anything contrary to the scriptures, you are calling God a liar. People are the varying factor, not God. I know you will see healing if you are persistent in your search. Remember, everyone is going to die, but you do not need to die sick.

Matthew 17:19-20 Then the disciples came to Jesus privately and said, "Why could we not cast it out?" So Jesus said to them, "Because of your unbelief, for assuredly, I say to you, if you have faith as a mustard seed, you will say to this mountain, 'Move from here to there,' and it will move; and nothing will be impossible for you.

Matthew 9:27-30 When Jesus departed from there, two blind men followed Him, crying out and saying, "Son of David, have mercy on us!" And when He had come into the house, the blind men came to Him. And Jesus said to them, "Do you believe that I am able to do this?" They said to Him, "Yes, Lord." Then He

touched their eyes saying, "According to your faith let it be done to you." And their eyes were opened...

Romans 1:17 For in it the righteousness of God is revealed from faith to faith; as it is written, "The just shall live by faith."

Everyone has faith. You do not need more faith, just less doubt. To get your faith to work for you and drown out doubt, you need to hear the message of God. Get in the word! Position yourself for victory, get baptized in the Holy Spirit. All instructions are contained in the bible for a victorious life in every area. You must believe in your heart. Do not mix doubt with your faith. Remember, Jesus said, "Only believe." I have not fully mastered this in every area of my life, but I am moving forward. Your confidence will grow with each answered prayer.

Romans 10:9-10 That if you confess with your mouth, "Jesus is Lord," and believe in your heart that God raised Him from the dead, you will be saved. For it is with your heart that you believe and are justified, and it is with your mouth that you confess and are saved.

Believe in your heart > Confess with your mouth > Receive the promise

Colossians 2:13-15 And you, being dead in your trespasses and the uncircumcision of your flesh, He made alive together with Him, having forgiven you all trespasses, having wiped out the handwriting of requirements that was against us, which was contrary to us. And He has taken it out of the way, having nailed it to the cross. Having disarmed principalities and powers, He made a public spectacle of them, triumphing over them in it.

My journey has lead me to the conclusion that if you believe with your whole heart that you are healed, confess with your mouth or speak to your mountain, you will not miss the mark. Doubt and unbelief were the only things that I could find in scripture that stop healing. Remember, doubt and unbelief have many faces; fear, anger, unforgiveness.

Don't wait until you are diagnosed with a terminal illness before you begin to exercise your faith. Start out with something small like a headache or stomachache. Command it to leave in the name of Jesus.

Practice believing what God says. Does your faith line up with your actions? If you are believing that you are well, get up and put your faith into action, don't act sick, don't mope around. The bible says, faith without works is dead. Example: If you have back pain and believe you are healed, bend over or do something that was difficult before. Look for the relief, not the pain.

Don't be a hearer only, but do what the word says. The word says to ONLY BELIEVE, resist the devil, forgive others, and love others.

In John 5:6 Jesus asked a man that had been sick for thirty-eight years if he wanted to be well. The man didn't answer with a yes or a no, he answered by giving excuses why he couldn't be well. Do you want to be well? This may seem like a silly question, but I believe after some people have had an illness for many years, they begin to believe it is part of their identity. I have heard people call fibromyalgia, "My fibromyalgia." We are not who our sickness is. We are who Jesus says we are.

You have to decide just how much you are going to tolerate from the devil. If you are sick and tired of being sick and tired, and you want to be well, you can be well. If you do not see instant results, don't give up. To believe in your heart, meditate on the truth. It may take more than reading a book or scripture once. Be diligent in your search and receive the reward. Don't limit God with unbelief and doubt.

LAST THOUGHTS:

Jesus loves you!

God's will is for us to be well!

Sickness is bad!

Healing is good!

Seek healing, not sickness!

Believe the right report!

Only believe!

Speak to your mountain!

Confess with your mouth!

Pray with authority, don't beg!

See and imagine yourself well!

Expect answers to your prayers after praying!

Everybody has thoughts, make your thoughts obey God's word!

Don't tolerate something that is not God's best for you!

1 Corinthians 15:57 But thanks be to God, who gives us victory through our Lord Jesus Christ.

NEED ADDITIONAL COPIES?

To order more copies of the book:

Only Believe ~ Amazing Grace

OR

To order the companion study guide:

Only Believe ~ Amazing Grace Study Guide

Contact:

- Amazon.com
- Create Space e Store

For questions about the book, contact:

mlpministries@yahoo.com

Made in the USA
San Bernardino, CA
29 May 2014